Reflections on ASEAN

Books by Mahathir Mohamad

Reflections on Asia
Malays Forget Easily
The Malaysian Currency Crisis
A New Deal for Asia
The Way Forward
The Challenges of Turmoil
The Voice of Asia: Two Leaders Discuss the Coming Century (*with Shintaro Ishihara*)
The Malaysian System of Government
Regionalism, Globalism and Spheres of Influence
The Challenge
Guide for Small Businessmen
The Malay Dilemma

Collected Speeches

Reflections on Asean
Terrorism and the Real Issues
Globalisation and the New Realities
Managing the Malaysian Economy
Politics, Democracy and the New Asia
Globalisation, Smart Partnership and Government
Islam and the Muslim Ummah
Regional Cooperation and the Digital Economy

Reflections on ASEAN

Selected Speeches of

DR MAHATHIR MOHAMAD

Prime Minister of Malaysia

Edited by

HASHIM MAKARUDDIN

Reflections on Asean
Selected Speeches of Dr Mahathir Mohamad
Prime Minister of Malaysia

Published by
Pelanduk Publications (M) Sdn Bhd
(Co. No. 113307-W)
12 Jalan SS13/3E, Subang Jaya Industrial Estate
47500 Subang Jaya, Selangor Darul Ehsan, Malaysia

for the
Prime Minister's Office of Malaysia
Putrajaya, Malaysia

Visit us at *www.pelanduk.com*
e-mail: *rusaone@tm.net.my*

Mahathir bin Mohamad, Tun, 1925-
Reflections on Asean / Mahathir Mohamad; edited by
Hashim Makaruddin.
Includes index
ISBN 967-978-884-9
1. Asia, Southeastern—Economic conditions. 2. Asia, Southeastern
—Politics and government. 3. Asia, Southeastern—Foreign relations.
4. Speeches, addresses, etc. I. Hashim Makaruddin. II. Title.
959

Printed and bound in Malaysia

Contents

Foreword

"I am also an Aseanist"

"I am a Malaysian nationalist. For this I offer no apologies. I am also an Aseanist. I am deeply committed to Asean, which has played such a critical role in turning what was an area of turmoil, antagonism, conflict—sometimes violent conflict, an area with no history of cooperation whatsoever, into a zone of cooperative peace and prosperity." (Dr Mahathir Mohamad at the Asia Society Conference on *Asia and the Changing World*, Tokyo, Japan, 1993)

WHEN one reads the following compilation of speeches on Asean by the Prime Minister of Malaysia, Dato' Seri Dr Mahathir Mohamad, from the time he assumed office on July 16, 1981 to his last farewell address at the 9th Asean Summit in Bali, Indonesia, in October 2003, one will be able to better appreciate the purport of the statement. It is not an empty statement. It is said in all sincerity and earnestness befitting the character of the man. It comes from a leader of Asean who has ruled the longest and has seen Asean go through various vicissitudes of fortune over the last two decades.

On another occasion, he emphasised that "in so far as Malaysia is concerned, Asean remains in the forefront of our foreign-policy priorities. The rationale behind the Malaysia government's thinking in this regard is the vital role of Asean as a stabilising influence and as a catalyst in developing the economic resilience of the region. We cannot prosper alone in a region that is in turmoil and unstable. To prosper we must have the kind of regional environment that is conducive to economic growth. Malaysia's adherence to the principles of Asean cooperation is therefore not altruistic. It is enlightened self-interest. And because it is so, we will always place the interest of Asean as a top priority." I have known of no other Asean leader who has made such a clear and categorical statement on the importance of Asean to his country.

I have also not known of any other Asean leader who has shown as consistently as Mahathir has his understanding, compassion, commitment and concern for Asean. All this comes out clearly in the speeches he delivered both within and outside Asean. These speeches demonstrate his continuous call for a stable and cohesive Asean, his caring attitude towards the well-being and the prosperity of the Asean peoples and his concern over Asean succumbing to pressures from outside.

As a visionary and a strategist, he is always full of ideas and suggestions on how Asean can face the challenges and the issues of the day. Some of these may appear far-fetched. However, as he himself explains it, "all important projects start as dreams in the minds of men of vision. We may or may not see our dream materialise, but if the objective is good and worthwhile, we should not be deterred by the magnitude or the problems."

In his speeches, Mahathir does not appear to preach or give "pep talks" as to what has gone wrong with Asean or why. Nor is there any hint that he is gloating over the misery of others. To him, "Leadership in Asean has most often meant leadership in sensitivity and consideration for others, in wisdom, in effort, in responsibility and in sacrifice—not leadership in dictating decisions and reaping benefits."

He has always called a spade a spade. I remember the times in the Foreign Ministry when it used to be pointed out to him that a particular part of his speech may not go down well with certain parties and he would reply with a wry smile that he will say what he has to say and be painted as the bad guy while we diplomats could appear to be the good guys! He has that uncanny ability, rarely found among leaders, to dissect difficult and intricate problems and concepts and present them in a coherent, rational and logical manner clear enough for the layman to understand. "Vintage Mahathir" was often a comment heard in reaction to his major speeches. One could fault him for his bluntness and what sometimes appear to be acrid comments at the gross inequalities and double standards in the international economic and political order, but one could not question his integrity or firm belief in what he says.

In this, Mahathir differed from his colleagues for most of them would rather shy away from controversy, least of all cause offence to any third party. Their speeches had a more "U.N.-esque" touch in that they were usually a tour of the political and socioeconomic scenario of Asean. They would look over the proceeding period since their last meeting and comment on the various issues, stating their governments' positions on them. They would, for instance, touch on the Treaty of Amity and Cooperation, the Zone of Peace, Freedom and Neutrality, the Southeast Asia Nuclear Weapons-Free Zone, the South China Sea, the Asean Regional Forum (ARF), AFTA, APEC, Asean and the WTO, with varying degrees of emphasis. There would also be calls on the need for greater Asean solidarity and cohesiveness in the face of daunting challenges facing Asean, together with the need for deepening and widening of Asean cooperation in the social and cultural fields and on such transnational issues as drugs, crime and the environment. A few leaders would have a variation to this approach and would go to the extent of decrying Asean's lack of progress and warn of Asean being left behind if the pace of inter-Asean cooperation was not intensified or speeded up.

For Mahathir, it was different. He would go to the heart of the matter and speak his mind. In that sense, he was the voice and conscience of Asean. He was the *de facto* spokesman of and for Asean. This is not to say that the other Asean leaders did not speak out on issues affecting Asean. But it was Mahathir who got the limelight and media attention. His media conferences were usually packed with standing room only for many and he would parry with them, question after question. The media loved him for it. There was no denying that a media conference by Mahathir was one which few would want to miss. Of course, the media would put its own spin on what he said in the news dispatches. As far as Mahathir was concerned, at least he was able to get his message across.

Each decade presented a different set of problems and challenges for Asean. In the 1980s, when Mahathir had just assumed office, Asean's economic cooperation was still in its infancy. Kampuchea and the problems of the boatpeople were its main preoccupation. These were compounded by the recession, the collapse of commodity prices and currency devaluation. This period saw Mahathir call for Asean countries to work more closely with each other, increase intra-Asean trade, set up commodity associations so that Asean could bargain from a position of strength. He repeated his calls for leaders to put Asean interests before all else and for a greater and more active role by the private sector.

To the outside world, his message was that Asean was really a sound place for investment, that it was ready to become a partner in development. He did not want Asean to be merely a "storehouse for commodities" and suggested diversification into manufacturing. He proposed the relocation of industries from Japan to Asean to take advantage of the lower costs of production and the establishment of "halfway houses" in Asean from where value-added products could be exported to third countries. He called protectionism as "morally wrong or harmful" and expressed fears about Europe becoming more inward-looking.

The 1990s opened with high hopes for a peace dividend as the Cold War came to an end. Within Asean, the Kampuchea question was finally settled and overtures came from Vietnam to join the Asean fraternity. This she did in 1995. Two years later, Laos and Myanmar joined on the 30th Anniversary of Asean, celebrated in Kuala Lumpur through a process in which Mahathir played a key role at a time when some Asean leaders appeared to be giving in to pressures from outside powers. Cambodia completed the

Asean-10 in 1999. The former battlefields were being turned to marketplaces.

It was the golden period of Asean when countries were growing at double-digit figures and FDI was flooding into Asean. It was the time when AFTA was initiated, marking the first concrete step taken towards greater integration of the region. The ARF was also established at this time to provide peace and security in the region. The ranks of the dialogue partners had swelled to 10 with the inclusion of China, India and Russia, adding stature and weight to the dialogue process in Asean and the ARF. This was the era of the "miracle growth" of "dragons" and "tigers". It was also the time when Mahathir had proposed the establishment of the East Asian Economic Grouping (EAEG), encompassing Asean, China, South Korea and Japan, to foster closer cooperation and interdependence of the Asean and East Asian regions.

During this period, Mahathir continued to call for a strong and united Asean to be able to shape the international economic and political order. He viewed the EAEG as the answer to the growing importance of the EEC and NAFTA. He argued strongly against the U.S.'s efforts at denying East Asians their right to build a platform for closer cooperation. He firmly believed that the Asean+3 would develop because of its "sound logic". He also opposed the linking of non-trade issues such as democracy, human and labour rights and environment as added conditionalities imposed upon the Newly Industrialised Countries (NICs) such as those in Asean and considered them as another guise for protectionism. He was also critical of those promoting democracy. He said "it is not democracy which is at fault but failure to understand it and, worse still, the manipulation of democracy by self-serving people". He spoke and wrote extensively on the phenomenon of globalisation and emphasised the need to inculcate the virtues of Asian values in the young in Asean.

When the Asian financial crisis devastated the region and decimated its economies, Mahathir was practically alone in his criticisms of the attempts to destabilise the currencies of the region through the "dictatorship of international manipulators." He also took to task the IMF and the World Bank which he said were manipulating the economies of the countries affected by the crisis. He was suggesting again for Asean countries to buy from one another what they were importing from outside. He called for barter trade and for the devaluation of the currencies simultaneously so as to increase trade among Asean countries. He highlighted the plight of the newer members of Asean, saying, "Poor neighbours are no asset to anyone. The problems of the poor are likely to spill over in the form of refugees, smuggling, black markets, etc. Poor countries are not good trading partners. Helping neighbours to become prosperous is therefore mutually beneficial."

Many of these issues have been carried over into the new millennium and continue to be the focus of attention and discussion in Asean. The issues of terrorism and its equation with Islam by some has caused much concern in Asean. It is an issue on which Mahathir's views have been sought extensively, being a moderate leader of an Islamic nation. He has spoken more extensively on this at other fora.

Looking at the speeches as a whole, it can be seen that Mahathir has been extremely busy and very involved on every issue Asean has faced in the last two decades of its existence. His departure will create a void that will be hard to fill. It will be difficult to find an

Aseanist as articulate as Mahathir, nor one who can make Asean the cornerstone of his country's foreign policy, an aspect he highlighted again in his farewell speech in Bali in October 2003.

Perhaps Indonesian President Megawati Sukarnoputri expressed it more eloquently on behalf of all member countries of Asean when presenting Mahathir a farewell gift from his colleagues at the Bali Summit:

> "It is a strange kind of farewell that we are bidding him. The mark of his personal statesmanship has been imprinted so deep in our consciousness that in a larger sense, he will always be with us.
>
> "The reach of his mind is so far and wide that on every issue laid before us we will always try to recall what Dr Mahathir said about it.
>
> "He always had strong and informed views, and never hesitated to say the unpleasant.
>
> "There is no way of counting the things he did for Asean. Indeed, he was one of those who worked the hardest to articulate Asean's vision of itself. That is why I can say with confidence that Dr Mahathir may leave office, but he will never abandon involvement with Asean."

Tan Sri Dato' Ajit Singh
Secretary-General of Asean
(January 1993-December 1997)
Kuala Lumpur, Malaysia
October 15, 2003

1

Asean's Commitment to Growth and Stability

"We in Asean strongly believe that the strength and stability of a country depends not so much on its armed forces but more importantly on our ability to intensify economic development and provide a better quality of life for our people."

THIS Asean-U.S. Economic Conference, to my mind, is a very important gathering. The idea to convene this meeting which came up early in 1980 has now become a reality not too long after the decision was taken. This only indicates the commitment and seriousness that both parties, the Asean side and the U.S. side, view the potentials of their

---

A speech delivered at the Asean-U.S. Economic Conference in Kuala Lumpur, Malaysia, on November 18, 1981

interaction and cooperation for mutual gain and benefit. Gathered here today are many prominent and influential people from the Asean countries and the U.S. representing the business sector as well as the government. In this modern age life has become so complex that it is impossible to demarcate between what is purely business and what is a public issue. Government cannot function without some business involvement and business needs government more and more, even when the free enterprise system is wholly espoused. Thus your presence, the representatives of the various fields of the private sector as well as the officials of the relevant agencies of the governments can go a long way towards making this Conference a success. All of us are very well aware of the need to transform the world economic order so as to arrive at a more truly just and equitable situation for the benefit of both the developing and the developed nations. I believe that for such a system to evolve there must be sincerity on all sides. This sincerity must not be just a word in the dictionary of conventional diplomacy for what is really sophisticated arm-twisting and manipulative endeavour for achieving more advantage by the already advantaged. What we need today if we are to achieve some semblance of a fair distribution of international wealth is sincerity based on true friendship and a clear understanding of the moral obligations that we all have towards each other. It is sad that after years of talking of a New International Economic Order we have achieved very little beyond talking. More of such talk, even if heads of State and heads of government are involved will not get us very far. What we need is sincere dialogue based on a firm commitment to resolve issues and solve problems. The political will to cooperate must be clearly laid down, so that officials and businessmen who are really involved in the day to day running of the economies of the world can than translate the ideas to promote the common good into reality on the ground.

It is in this light that I feel your meeting is an important and meaningful effort in helping to improve and institutionalise a better system and framework for cooperation between nations. For us in Asean, cooperation is the key to our future. It is in the best interest of every Asean country to see to Asean's success as a group. We do not claim that we do not have problems or for that matter differences among us; we have learnt that through goodwill and cooperation we can achieve at least part of the goals that we have set for us. Today we see increasing cooperation not just at the level of officials but among the professionals and the people in general. Our cooperation with third countries is also bearing fruits. In fact, your meeting is a result of this new and increasing understanding and spirit of cooperation between Asean and third countries, whether singly or as groups.

I need not dwell at length on Asean as an entity. I am sure most of you are acquainted with this region. Asean's strategic location, its economic resources and potentials, and above all, the region's commitment to free enterprise and the market economy are not unfamiliar. With a population of more than 250 million people, stable governments, a responsive work force and with abundant natural resources, we possess the necessary ingredients to stimulate a more vigorous economic growth. The political and economic stability in the Asean countries are indeed remarkable assets considering the general tendency towards instability of the region as a whole. This stability is no fluke. It has been worked at. And countries which can work towards the achievement of such stability must be considered reliable by those venturing from outside the region.

One of Asean's primary concern is the maintenance of peace and stability in this region. This concern is reflected in our efforts to create a Zone of Peace, Freedom and Neutrality (ZOPFAN) in Southeast Asia. We believe that it is only through peace and stability that we in the region could devote more time and effort in the pursuit of economic and social development. We in Asean strongly believe that the strength and stability of a country depends not so much on its armed forces but more importantly on our ability to intensify economic development and provide a better quality of life for our people. In this day and age, wars of conquests are no longer fashionable. Countries are subjugated through internal upheavals. We in Asean are acutely aware of the need to remove the causes of such upheavals. Our economic policies and development are designed so as to contribute towards political stability. Pure economic accomplishments without regard for the welfare and desires of the people has been shown to be a destabilising factor and even a cause of the downfall of governments. Thus, our economic policies are based on clear and definite political objectives. If we impose conditions on foreign investors, it is not because we grudge you your profits, but because we have a need to reconcile foreign economic incursions with national aspirations. In the long run, the political stability we achieve is for you, much more worthwhile commercially than the short-term profits you might make.

Next to political stability, Asean values highly the need to maintain economic growth with price stability. As a matter of economic philosophy, Asean believe that the objective of stable economic growth can best be achieved in an environment of free enterprise in a market economy. Private investment, both domestic and foreign, is encouraged to expand and to seek new opportunities to raise productive capacity in the region. We encourage the private sector to achieve greater profitability through higher productivity. In return, we expect investors and entrepreneurs to be responsible corporate citizens.

The role of governments in Asean is centred on maintaining a stable economic environment. We learn a lot from each other and consequently there a great deal of similarity in the policies on economic growth pursued by Asean countries. One of the things that we know investors value highly is predictability. Consequently since the formation of Asean we have avoided making sudden tangential departures from set courses. We do not nationalise, for example. However, if you sell your shares in the market we pertaining to economic policies is our asset. It has contributed to a stable economic environment. Apart from this we have invested heavily in education and training. The productivity of our work force is accordingly high. At least three of the Asean nations are able to export highly trained labour. But as Asean progresses their workers will come back to help with the development of their countries.

Strong governments are also characteristic of Asean countries and this must enhance economic stability. Sudden ideological changes are not our style. We are all committed to promote stable growth with equity.

The world is passing through a most difficult economic period. Recovery does not seem to be within sight yet. The recession in the industrialised nations naturally has a debilitating effect on the economy of the producers of primary commodities like the majority of Asean countries. In an attempt to get away from overdependence on a few primary commodities, we have started to diversify and industrialise. Efforts at agricultural diversification have made us more resilient; but, the moment we begin to take advantage of our international comparative advantage position to move downstream and process more and more of our primary produce for export, the markets in the major industrial countries begin to change the rules of the game. Now our industrialisation programme is being held up because global recession does not enable us to earn enough from our primary commodities. Also we are not able to sell the few manufactured products which we have been able to produce efficiently and at competitive prices because of increased protectionist sentiments in the developed nations.

These external factors make the job of maintaining economic stability by the Asean governments very difficult. For us, the conduct of international trade has become a game of tails I lose and heads you win. Furthermore, we are dismayed at the slow progress on the part of the major industrial countries to get out of their recession and combat inflation. With the exception of Japan, they appear to be caught in the web of high interest rates, high consumer prices, high wage demands, low investment, low productivity and low or no growth. In our growing interdependent world, their continuing stagflation generates a general malaise in world trade and growth, to the detriment of the least developed nations which can ill-afford to be confronted with such a situation. Worse, much of the high inflation is exported to the developing countries, thereby adding to their gloom.

Taking all these into consideration, it is remarkable that the Asean countries have been able to maintain fairly steady and comparatively high growth in real terms. There may be many factors contributing to this stability of economic growth but it will not be wrong to say that there is a strong element of good management of Asean governments and their policies. This by itself should again be a plus for foreigners doing business with Asean.

The liberal attitude of the Asean governments is yet another factor in the growth and stability of the Asean countries. Funds flow fairly freely in and out of Asean countries. There are regulations, of course, but they are minimal as compared with other developing countries. Consequently the fear over the recovery of capital or profits does not deter investors. The nett result is a greater inflow of funds and technology which contribute towards growth and economic stability.

The Asean countries are the original Spice Islands of history. European nations fought wars in order to have access to the spices of the Spice Islands. Today, Asean it is not only a leading producer of spices but provide the world with 91 per cent of natural rubber, 87 per cent of tin, 88 per cent of palm oil, 73 per cent of copra, and 62 per cent of tropical hardwood apart from petroleum, copper, abaca and cocoa. In addition, there is a vast hydroelectric potential. Clearly the Asean countries have tremendous resources. The world is welcome to these resources, but while wars of conquests are no longer necessary in order to get at them, good commercial practices are still valuable.

The Asean countries naturally do not want to be merely storehouses for commodities. They want to add value to commodity base is processed or manufactured in the region. In order to derive the maximum benefit from the production of raw materials, Asean has definite plans to attract joint ventures in the processing and manufacture of raw materials on a large scale. Relatively cheaper labour and other overheads as well as abundant resources and numerous investment incentives should make such industries very worthwhile indeed.

Political stability, predictability, sustained and whether foreign or local. Clearly Asean is a good bet for progressive and forward looking businessmen. Already those who have come and invested are reaping rich harvests. Some Asean countries, like Malaysia for example, have become significant exporters of components for high technology products like computers as a result of foreign investments. Exports of electrical products are also on the increase. Our effectiveness in the export of resource-based manufactures has begun to make inroads in even the most competitive international markets.

The emphasis on resource-based industries imply continuing reliance on imported capital goods. The Asean nations are not intending to compete with the developed countries. Rather they wish to complement. And as their prosperity increases with economic growth they will provide rich markets for the goods of the industrialised nations.

Import accounts for no less than one-third of the GNP of the Asean countries. In one or two the ratio is much higher. In the 1970s, Asean imports expanded at about 23 per cent annually, financed mainly by its equally rapidly rising exports, which rose by an average 25 per cent a year, and by abundant private savings. Reflecting this buoyant situation, growth in productive capacity had also accelerated. Fixed investments rose at an annual rate of between 20 and 23 per cent in the

1970s. This dynamic process has been sustained so far in the 1980s.

This being an Asean affair I would not like to speak much about Malaysia. A few words about this least known of Asean partners are however not out of place, I think.

Malaysia has been a very consistent exponent of all the policies of Asean. Indeed, long before Asean was mooted, Malaysia has already made clear its belief in the free enterprise system and its welcome for foreign investors. Consequently, steady economic growth has been a characteristic of Malaysia almost since independence in 1957.

This economic achievement of Malaysia is that much more noteworthy considering that Malaysia is plagued by a number of intractable internal problems. Foremost among them is the unequal development of the component races in Malaysia's multiracial society. To reduce this inequality requires active steps by the government. Thus in the early 1970s the New Economic Policy (NEP) was adopted with the twin objectives of eradicating poverty irrespective of race and the restructuring of society so as to eliminate the identification of race with economic function. Both these thrusts are essentially economic. Consequently the growth of the economy has to be subjected to some restrain. Yet, despite these fairly considerable constraints Malaysia's real economic growth has been maintained for many years at the rate of approximately 8 per cent. And this growth has been achieved without significant inflation.

The NEP is in the interest not only of Malaysians but also foreign investors. It has enabled the political climate to remain stable, thus preventing the wild changes of policies that are so damaging to business, and also preventing the kind of disruptive activities that people under political tension are prone to.

Malaysia is ruled by conservatives whose only desire is to develop the country for the benefit of the people. Radicalism and extremism has been rejected not only by the government but also by the people. There are of course extremists and fanatics but they have not been able to make headway among the masses. There is consequently little fear of anti foreign agitations of the kind seen in some countries. However, it does not mean that Malaysians don't have national pride or they are not sensitive. They are likely to be peeved if you say they live on trees.

Malaysia at the moment is diversifying her economy so as to be free from excessive dependence on the production of raw materials. An industrialisation programme, which started almost as soon as independence was achieved has gained momentum steadily. This programme is quite dependent on foreign participation. Certain rules and regulations have been formulated so that while the foreign investors are not deprived of their profits, Malaysia and Malaysians fully benefit from the process of industrialisation. The latest move is into heavy industries and high technology industries. With little indigenous expertise, the participation of foreigners is even more welcome in these areas. Of course, Malaysia expects a significant transfer of technology in the process.

How successful these programmes and policies are, you can see for yourself. Kuala Lumpur is a bustling capital where once it was a sleepy colonial administrative centre. What you see in Kuala Lumpur you will see all over Malaysia, from Kota Kinabalu in Sabah to Kangar in Perlis. The government has deliberately spread out the development so that there is even growth. Locational incentives are used to achieve this.

I hope that this rapid sketch of Malaysia and its potentials is not out of place here. However, it would be a pity if I left you without saying a few words about inflation in Malaysia, even though much of this is imported. Although inflation is fashionable today, it is quite an alien experience for us. We had managed to grow strongly up to the early 1970s with an average rate of inflation of only about 1 per cent annually. For the most part of the 1970s, inflation was less than 5 per cent a year. But, we are realistic enough to recognise that so long as the industrial nations continue to inflate at a high rate, we will have to deal with it squarely. As a matter of public policy, inflation will be controlled and reduced progressively. We intend to have a firm grip here through fiscal and monetary discipline. We have many things going for us: the economy saves 25-30 per cent on the GNP; monetary expansion is kept consonant with output growth; we balance our current budget and whatever surpluses we have, together with the traditional but reliable flow of private savings with specialised institutions, are normally sufficient to finance the bulk of our development programmes. Whenever we need to supplement these funds, we borrow from abroad. Because we do so infrequently, our external debt servicing ratio is at present only about 2 per cent of our export earnings. No matter what happens, we are determined to ensure that world inflation will not engulf us. I am sure you will agree that this is good for business.

2

Asean: A Regional Approach Towards Stability

"But Asean has shown that although it is not a military grouping, it can coordinate its policies so as to deter the kind of adventures that countries standing alone and economically troubled attract."

WHEN the United Nations (U.N.) was formed in 1945, the world felt that an agency had been found for the resolution of conflicts between nations. The failure of the League of Nations was forgotten in the euphoria that greeted the emergence of the United Nations Organisation (UNO). In the

---

A speech delivered at the Asia Society and the Council of Foreign Relations in New York, United States, on September 28, 1982

colonised territories like the states of the Malay peninsula, hope was kindled that freedom and dignity were once again attainable. Such were the expectations in Malaysia that the most popular political party among the Malays, which today governs Malaysia as part of a coalition, was named after the United Nations Organisation. The United Malays National Organisation (UMNO), of which I am the current President, drew a lot of inspiration and saw a lot of similarities between the Malay states and the United Nations as a concept.

In a sense those expectations were justified. We believe that the Empires of the first half of the 20th century would not have been broken up nor new countries created but for the United Nations. Unfortunately, the break-up of the Empires was not to result in real freedom for the emergent nations. The metropolitan powers were too powerful and too far advanced for the new nations to establish relations on equal footing. Indirectly they continue to dominate their former colonies. As if this is not enough the old countries of Europe formed an alliance which uses economic power to continue political domination. The U.S. too was drawn into this grouping, thus adding strength to the domination of European countries over their former colonies.

The European Economic Community (EEC) is, of course, not a new idea. Alliances between neighbours have been known throughout the history of mankind. But the EEC is perhaps the first alliance to focus on economic cooperation. This is perhaps because the North Atlantic Treaty Organisation (NATO) already provides for military cooperation.

We see many weaknesses in the EEC. Indeed, some say it is a failure. But a Europe competing with itself would probably be worse off than the EEC. The EEC as a Regional Grouping can therefore be said to be successful. In any case Regional Groupings of countries caught on. Thus a spate of regional groupings was formed in the Caribbean, in Africa, the Arab countries, Eastern Europe and in Southeast Asia. Now, of course, South Asia is interested. as a case study and discuss it in the context of stability through regional grouping. I do not think I will be able to say much that is not already known, but I cannot possibly know how much you already know. So if what I say is old hat to you, I must crave your indulgence.

We like to think that when we do something, we know all the objectives and the consequences. But this is far from the truth. Usually, our foresight is quite limited and within a short while after we are off on a supposedly planned course, we will find so many difficulties and so many unforeseen things that we wonder why we never foresaw these contingencies. Indeed, sometimes we are reduced to cursing our own stupidity in embarking on a plan or a course of action.

This is true of Asean—particularly in the eyes of others. While the actual planners had fairly limited objectives, others infer all kinds of Machiavellian strategies in the concept of Asean that they tended to believe that the regional grouping has fallen far short of its target. Thus we find outsiders cynically commenting on the failure of Asean as an economic community, when in fact economic cooperation was not a prime objective of the early Asean leaders.

I would like to say this. Asean is not a Machiavellian concept. Asean was conceived as a simple forum to overcome the communications problem between neighbours who then knew little about each other. The five countries of Asean are ethnically similar, but historically and politically diverse. Malaysia and Singapore were once ruled by the British, and that association affected the values, the system of government and the general outlook. Indonesia was ruled by the Dutch and again the Dutch mould affected the Indonesians and physically separated them from their cousins across the Straits of Malacca. The Philippines was both Spanish and American, and they felt so divorced from the other countries of Southeast Asia that in the eyes of some people, they could hardly be considered Southeast Asian. It is the only Christian (Catholic) country in a region peopled by Muslims and Buddhists. Then, of course, there is Thailand, the only Southeast Asian country which was not colonised; is a kingdom that modernised and had direct relations with Europe—when its neighbours were being colonised. The Thai's knowledge of the newly independent neighbours was minimal.

It can thus be seen that suddenly five historically separated countries found themselves having to conduct relations not as familiar neighbours but as suspicious strangers. It would be a miracle if they do not mess up their relations. And indeed this was what happened initially. Within a very short space of time, they were in confrontation. Territorial claims were made and threats uttered. At one stage, the Sukarno regime actually dropped paratroopers on Malaysian territory.

To cut a long story short, the leaders of these countries decided to meet each other to thrash out their neighbourhood problems. Despite the differences, it did not take long for the idea of a neighbourhood association to be proposed as a forum for solving the usual problems between neighbours. Thus, we first had the Association of Southeast Asia (ASA). The proponents involved then were only Malaysia, Thailand and the Philippines. Singapore was then a part of Malaysia while Thailand was not a party to the Confrontation by President Sukarno. Despite some agreement on the need for this grouping, ASA never really took off. But nevertheless, the get-together was found to be useful as a forum for amicable settlement of the differences between neighbours. Though ASA failed to achieve the settlement, the concept remained in the minds of Southeast Asian leaders. And, finally when the Indonesian Confrontation ended, the idea of a regional grouping came to the forefront again.

It can be seen that it was not economic cooperation that was the motive behind the formation of Asean. Certainly, it was not a strategic concept designed to make the five Asean nations an economic and political entity which will overawe its neighbours and present a mutual front in the international fora. Asean is simply a fairly ad hoc solution to a communications problem between neighbours who were strangers to each other. But once it was formed, much more was expected of it than was ever in the minds of the founders. It is this expectation that makes Asean seem to fall short of its objective. On the other hand, looked at from the limited aims of the founders, it is a success.

Now let us examine the achievements of Asean. When I was asked to deliver the keynote speech at a forum on the Pacific Basin in Bali, I emphasised the need to know each other better before real cooperation can take place. With the formation of Asean, the strangers who peopled the neighbouring countries of Southeast Asia began to know each other well. Certainly the leaders became very friendly with one another. In fact, one of the characteristics of Asean meetings is that most of the work and the process of reaching consensus are achieved during informal get-togethers of ministers in the absence of their official advisers.

When people are that close to each other, they cannot but learn from each other. It is an acknowledged fact that the Asean-5 have achieved remarkable progress in a world where economic growth has become very limited. This achievement in terms of economic growth is not an accident. It is made possible by the policies followed by the Asean nations, policies which were devised through learning from each other the formula for success. At one time prior to Asean, there were countries of Southeast Asia which were tempted to be ultra-nationalistic economically. Foreign holdings were forcibly nationalised. But learning from the other Asean countries that such was not the route to prosperity, nationalisation was dropped. All the Asean countries are now believers in free trade and free enterprise. Foreign capital is welcome by all. Incentives for investments are common. Joint ventures are popular. On the other hand, Indonesia taught the new Southeast Asian oil-producing countries how to bargain with foreign oil companies.

Clearly the first and greatest achievement of Asean is the exchange of mutual experience and administrative know-how which have led to economic growth and stability. Today, the Asean-5 are prosperous and stable—relative to the rest of the world, and certainly relative to the newly independent countries elsewhere.

But all these are not noticed or at least are not regarded as Asean achievements. In the eyes of foreigners in particular, Asean has failed because it has not been able to set up a common market. But as I have explained earlier, a common market was not what

Asean leaders had in mind when they decided to form the grouping. It was only after the group was formed that people began to talk of on Asean common market. The reason is that people immediately think of the EEC when they see such a grouping. For a lot of people, next to security, economic power is the only reason for a grouping of neighbours. Foreign businessmen see in a grouping of countries a solution to the problem of dealing with many countries, each with its own laws and peculiarities. How much more simple it will be for them if they can gain entry into a five-nation market through one country that they are familiar with. And so they watch hopefully for evidence that the customs barriers between the Asean countries would be brought down. But although thousands of items have now been accorded preferential tariffs, a real breakdown of customs barriers has not taken place. Asean is therefore a failure in the eyes of these people.

But local business people entertain different ideas. The Asean member with a small domestic market like Singapore would like to remove tariff barriers. But the Indonesian businessmen and the government would like to retain the potential of a 150 million population for themselves. So would Thailand and the Philippines, each with a population of about 45 million. Malaysia is neither here nor there. With a population of only over 14 million, it still manages to have the biggest passenger car market among the Asean-5.

It is comparatively a more affluent market.

For the local business people and the governments of Asean countries, there is no great hurry to lift tariff barriers. The economic strength of each country must be built up first before they open the floodgates. It is hoped that at such a time, the flow will not be in one direction only. The benefits must be mutual.

In many ways, therefore, it can be said that Asean as a regional grouping is a success. Certainly it has brought prosperity and stability. There remains the threat to stability from non-member neighbours. But Asean has shown that although it is not a military grouping, it can coordinate its policies so as to deter the kind of adventures that countries standing alone and economically troubled attract.

Among the kind of cooperation that is designed by Asean to ward off threats is the concept of a Zone of Peace, Freedom and Neutrality (ZOPFAN). This concept requires the cooperation of the big powers. That cooperation is not really forthcoming, but each of the big powers is not willing to say that they disapprove of peace or of freedom or of neutrality in Southeast Asia. In a sort of negative way, ZOPFAN is working.

For the purpose of security, the Asean countries depend The capacity of Asean countries to do this no doubt contributes to the dampening of external pressures and threats.

In the case of Asean, it can be said that regional grouping has had positive results in terms of economic cooperation itself. It depends more upon the willingness to know and understand each other and, accepting the shortcomings, to work within the constraints. No grand design should be tried purely because it sounds good or it had worked elsewhere.

3

Europeans Can Invest in Asean with Confidence

"... whatever has developed to date in respect of Asean is merely the tip of the iceberg. Whatever you see as potential for today is only a small fraction of the future potential that this region will offer to manufacturers who have the vision and the faith to see the progress of Asean and to take advantage of what we have to offer now."

IT gives me great pleasure to be here today in conjunction with this first Asean-EEC Industrial Sectoral Conference to be held in this region to promote the increased flow of direct investments into

---

A speech delivered at the Asean-EEC Industrial Sectoral Conference in Kuala Lumpur, Malaysia, on February 28, 1983

sectors of industry that are vital to the development of the region.

It is appropriate that this Conference is held during this period when both developed and developing countries are slowly staggering to their feet, trying to overcome the onslaught of the global recession that has affected all our economies. Needless to say, different countries have fought the effects of the recession with varying degrees of success. Some have had to contend with zero or negative growth rates while others have had to be satisfied with very marginal growth. However, if one looks at the performance on a global basis during this dismal period in the economic history of the world, one cannot but notice that there is one region that has maintained growth at a significant level; and that is the Asean region.

It was said by a leading European personality some time ago that the centre of gravity of economic growth is shifting slowly from the West to the East and especially to the Asean region. I feel that there is no better proof of the veracity of this statement than the fact that all the Asean countries have generated, are generating and will apparently continue to generate positive growth rates during these difficult times.

The European Economic Community represents a regional grouping of nations that has for long exerted considerable economic influence on world trade and investments. Some members of the EEC, have in the past had a role as the colonial masters of some of the Asean countries. The EEC has unfortunately also used its collective strength to deprive Asean and other developing nations from a share of the rich markets in Europe, even for manufactured products that are based on the natural resources of these developing nations. I make this statement to you because we need to face this truth if we are to make meetings such as this worthwhile.

In the past, members of the EEC, and indeed other developed nations, have been happy to keep the nations of Asean and other developing countries merely as suppliers of their requirements of raw commodities, both agricultural and mineral. Some of the Asean countries have found to their dismay, as other developing countries have found, that political independence which threw away the shackles of forced developing countries around the world to become intractable; seemingly engrossed with rhetoric and impossible demands without being able to demonstrate the practicality or logic of their stance. Even the regional groupings that they form seem at times devoid of credibility. Indeed, some of these groupings have perished. Asean is one of the very few to survive and to possess a viable economic and political programme.

With this background and an awareness of the near-collapse of the world economic system, we in the Asean region are very happy that the European Commission has taken the initiative to organise this sectoral conference as a follow-up to the general investment promotion seminars held earlier in Jakarta and in Brussels. I am sure I echo the emerging economic force of tomorrow—can only be engendered if there is genuine desire for the members of the EEC to assist in the fulfillment of the legitimate aspirations of the peoples and nations of Asean.

We most certainly do not want to continue to be the plantations and mines for Europe or the rest of the world. We most certainly do not cherish the dubious honour that Asean holds as a world leader in the production of various raw commodities whose prices are often dictated by the tender mercies of market manipulators and close-shop trading systems in Europe and other parts of the world. We most certainly do not want to see our peoples breaking their backs to till the soil and mine the land for depleting commodities, only to find that those who work the hardest are those who obtain the least economic benefits for their endeavours. Finally, we most certainly do not want to perpetuate our manufacturing sectors at the lower ranges of the scale of world technology.

We are most happy that the European Commission has recognised this and has organised this seminar that will examine the prospects for the manufacture of agricultural machineries, machine tools and processing machines in the Asean region. Malaysia would most certainly like to see some of these projects established in this country. However, as a member of Asean, we would like to see these projects materialise in any of the Asean countries, for wherever the location of the projects within Asean all the Asean nations will surely benefit. The beneficial multiplier effects of increased industrialisation and development within any country in the Asean region will be felt more closely in future by neighbouring Asean countries, than if such projects were established outside this region.

I will not allow myself, or my friends from the other Asean countries, to be deluded into believing that the manufacturers of these products from the EEC, having profitable operations there, will relocate their projects in the Asean region for the sake of friendship, etc. We have stopped believing in altruism long ago. What we in the Asean region offer to all industrialists from developed countries, including the EEC, is a region of stability and dynamic growth where you can invest with confidence and make reasonable profits from your investments while complying with the policies and needs of the host countries. economic battles that Japan is winning in the markets of Europe and in other international markets are being fought not merely from the shores of Japan, but from developing countries such as those in the Asean region. Today, for example, Malaysia is the world's third largest exporter of room air-conditioners because of Japanese manufacturing activities in this country; and this is only one example of the fertile grounds for profits that Asean has provided for those who are prepared to identify and commit themselves to the long-term economic interests of this region.

The need to be competitive in the international market for a whole range of lower, medium and high technology products dictates that companies in the developed countries, be it the EEC, the U.S. or Japan, must appreciate fully the laws of comparative advantage, long neglected because of unequal economic strengths and unfair practices engendered through tariff barriers. With the reality of increasing costs of raw materials, transportation, wages, etc., and the equally glaring reality of the need to bring down the prices of manufactured products if companies wish to remain competitive and to meet the demands of consumers, there is a need for manufacturers in the EEC to look towards countries such as those in the Asean region as partners for their future growth and profitability.

We in the Asean region recognise that industrialists from the EEC can make a valuable contribution to the progress of this region and to the welfare of the world in general. We are aware that your contribution in terms of technological know-how, management skills and export market outlets can help members of the Asean countries release the stranglehold of the cycle of low income, lack of capital and know-how and continuing low income that entrap most developing nations. Undoubtedly different members in the Asean region are in different stages of development in this respect, but collectively it is our aspiration to move into higher levels of technology that we know can be offered by the West.

However, we are equally aware that we offer the Western manufacturers a fertile ground for new investments, growth and profit in one of the fastest growing regions of the world. The market that we form, and potentially it is a rich market, is not there simply for you to exploit. But you may share that market if you are willing to share what you have in abundance, i.e., technological know-how, capital, management and marketing skills. And of course a portion of your own huge market must be open to the products that together we will manufacture.

All these remarks I address to the EEC collectively and to each and every industrialist in Europe who no doubt wish to expand and increase their activity and profits. But let me also leave these thoughts with the members of the European Commission and to all those in the private sector who have influence in the policy making levels in the governments of the EEC.

In the world today there has been a considerable amount of rhetoric on the dangers of protectionism. This subject has become the favourite theme of virtually all recent international gatherings, be it of politicians, economists or businessmen. And frequently those who most blatantly practise protectionism are the most vociferous in the condemnation of this policy.

Protectionism is, needless to say, contrary to free trade. When the Bretton Woods agreement was made the participants were the few countries which dominated the world at that time. They advocated free trade because to them it meant they could freely enter the markets of those countries not in a position to export products which can compete with their own. Today the picture has changed. The countries which in the immediate postwar period were mere markets are now the manufacturers and exporters of competitive goods. And these countries, having been persuaded that free trade is the ideal system, want to sell their goods freely in the industrially developed countries. Suddenly free trade takes on a different complexion for the formulators of the Bretton Woods agreement. And so free trade becomes a dirty word to be replaced by a newly salvaged protectionism.

It is clear that the practice of protectionism by the co-signatories of the Bretton Woods agreement is morally wrong. But more than that it is harmful. Free trade is still the ideal policy for our interdependent world. We we are going to need supplies or expertise or capital from outside. And when we are in that situation our protectionist attitude is not going to help. We are going to do if you find that you are unable to sell for cash what you produce.

A lot of people will say it is not going to work. And I am inclined to think that it will not work as well as free trade. But the choice is not between free trade and countertrade. The choice is between countertrade and no trade. In that situation countertrade will not only look good but it will give some results. And sufficient countertrade will succeed to damage the protectionists to some degree. The socialist countries with their preference for government-to-government deals will obviously find countertrade a good means of unloading the goods that they find so difficult to market. And once a practice becomes established it will be most difficult to dislodge it. The old contacts and symbiosis that existed between the interdependent free enterprise free trade world may disappear for good.

However, before interdependence disappears it is going to do its share of the damage. The recent fall in oil prices may be a cause for much rejoicing in the industrialised countries. No longer will they be held to ransom by the Organisation of Petroleum-Exporting Countries (OPEC). No longer will OPEC lord it over the world. But the banks which lent money to some third world countries and oil producers are going to suffer from the collapse of these countries. Already we see Mexico in dire straits dragging down with it not just the lending banks but damaging the economies of the developed countries as well.

Clearly then interdependence means interdependence. It does not mean dependence of the weak on the strong. It obviously does not mean dependence of the strong on the weak. It means that the weak and the strong must support each other in good times as in bad. It means that they must depend on each other. If the strong is rich, the weak will have a share of this wealth. Conversely if the strong becomes poor the weak will suffer. The effect of recession in the developed countries on the export revenues of countries like Malaysia is ample proof of this. On the other hand, if the weak are helped to become rich, then the strong will become richer from the markets that will open up.

I think it is worthwhile for the participants of this world is facing a recession. You also know that some of the developed countries are resorting to the wrong strategy to counter that recession. I hope that knowing this you will use your influence to force a halt to the protectionist inward looking policies that is aggravating an already dangerous situation. Let us all return to sanity and the ways that in the 1960s and 1970s brought prosperity to the world.

During the next two days I am sure you will be exposed to all the latest developments taking place in the Asean region and the benefits that each of these Asean countries can offer you. I would like to add only that whatever has developed to date in respect of Asean is merely the tip of the iceberg. Whatever you see as potential for today is only a small fraction of the future potential that this region will offer to manufacturers who have the vision and the faith to see the progress of Asean and to take advantage of what we have to offer now.

Many have said that the economic concepts within Asean are progressing very slowly. We say that we are progressing with "deliberate speed". We want to build a structure, brick by brick, so that the final edifice will stand the test of time. We do not want to act in haste just to satisfy our ego that we have got a great economic grouping, only to regret at leisure when we find the structure falling apart at the slightest stress. I must admit that we have learned a lot from the EEC itself in terms of mistakes to avoid, and paths to pursue or not to pursue, and thus we will continue to "make haste" cautiously. However, I would like to caution all potential investors not to be lulled into a sense of complacency because of the speed the various regional economic activities within Asean are progressing. The leaders of the Asean nations have committed themselves to policies and measures of economic cooperation designed to mutually lift the entire level of economic development within Asean. All those who come in now, will surely benefit from the fruits of our endeavours now and in the future.

4

Seeking New Frontiers for Sustained Growth

"... there is a critical need now for Asean to seek out new frontiers, in partnership with its immediate neighbours, to promote sustained growth since the old established industrial nations can no longer be relied upon exclusively to provide the engine of growth in world trade."

THIS meeting is timely because the growing importance of the Pacific region makes it imperative that Asean meet with the two giants which flank it to the north and the south, to ascertain how best to work together for mutual benefit. This meeting is also timely because there is a critical need now for

---

A speech delivered at the Economic Symposium organised by the *Australian Financial Review* and the *Nihon Keizai Shimbun* in Kuala Lumpur, Malaysia, on May 7, 1984

Asean to seek new frontiers and opportunities, in partnership with its immediate neighbours, to promote sustained growth since the old established industrial nations can no longer be relied upon exclusively to provide the engine of growth in world trade. During the recessionary period between 1981 and 1983, the Asean region demonstrated its dynamism by expanding its combined average GNP at close to 5 per cent in real terms annually. Most of the Asean economies are now on the way to resuming their pre-recession growth paths. What is important is to ensure that this growth process is sustained. The people in the Asean countries have come to expect this. Asean cannot allow world recession to adversely affect this growth. Even if there is the faintest possibility that economic interaction with countries like Japan and Australia will contribute towards Asean's economic health, this must be examined and worked at.

Asean is a major supplier of natural resources to the world. We produce and export the bulk of the world's supply of natural rubber, tin, tropical hardwoods, pepper, copra and palm oil. We are also a major producer and exporter of petroleum, gas, rice and other food products. In return, we buy manufactured products, especially from Japan. We are in a hurry to develop, to industrialise with the help of modern technology and to raise the standard of living of our people. It is our aim to become an important grouping of developed nations as soon as possible. To achieve this goal the Asean countries have tried to complement each others' effort. But this is not easy because the Asean countries have always been each others' competitors. Consequently intra-Asean trade has not been significant. Despite vigorous promotion, intra-Asean trade now accounts for only about 15 per cent of the total Asean trade with the world.

Until such time when the Asean countries learn to complement each other and increase the volume of intra-Asean trade, Asean will have to depend on the rest of the world for its market. For some time now the Asean countries have been trying to improve export performance by adding manufactured goods to the string of primary commodities that they export. But this has made no significant impact. As the pace of development increases, Asean imports of manufactured products keep on outstripping the value of the exports. In 1983 the combined trade deficit of the original Asean-5 was U.S.$11 billion. Even import restrain has not been able to reduce the adverse balance. To find an answer

Asean trade with Australia is small, amounting US$200 million in 1982. The bulk of Asean exports to Australia, totalling US$1.5 to $2 billion, is made up of primary commodities. About 60 per cent of Australia's imports from Asean comprised petroleum, mainly from Indonesia and Singapore. Excluding the petroleum trade, Asean's trade deficit would reach US$1.1 billion. However, Asean's manufactured exports accounted for only about 3 per cent of Australia's total imports of manufactured goods. On the other hand, Asean imports mainly food, manufactured goods, machinery and equipment from Australia.

Asean trade with Japan is far more significant. In 1982, about 25 per cent of the total trade of the original Asean-5 was with Japan. As a group, Asean had a trade surplus of US$800 million with Japan in 1982, due to the hefty surplus of Indonesia, mainly on account of petroleum exports. The other Asean members, namely Malaysia, the Philippines, Singapore and Thailand, all experienced deficits with Japan. The composition of this trade is a familiar story. We export mainly raw materials, largely unprocessed, and import a wide range of manufactured goods as well as plants and equipments. As in the case of Australia, Japan imports only a negligible amount of Asean manufactures.

It is quite clear that Asean's trading relationship with Japan and Australia requires review. Not only should the volume of trade between these close neighbours be increased but there should be greater balance in the trade. The trend that we see is that the balance would favour Australia even more when more coal and iron are bought for new plants in the Asean countries. As for Japan, with oil prices at present levels and manufactured goods not only continuing to increase in price but also increasing in variety and sophistication, the balance may change in favour of Japan in the near future.

So what can be done. If Australia and Japan would like to sell more to the Asean countries, they will have to help the Asean countries earn more foreign exchange. Obviously they will have to buy more from Asean. Commodities have low added value. An increase in the import of Asean commodities would not enrich the Asean countries much. But if those commodities are processed into manufactured goods and exported, the Asean countries would make substantial earnings. Malaysia for example, has ambitions to become the biggest producer of rubber tyres in the world. With the advantage of lower raw material and labour cost, together with the economies of scale possible for a world supplier, it is not impossible for Malaysia to capture a substantial portion of the world market. If for a start Australia and Japan buys tyres from Malaysia, then not only will the balance of payment be corrected, but the two countries will not be just importing raw materials from Malaysia. In addition, earnings from higher value exports would enable Malaysia to buy more goods from Japan and Australia. There is no way by which Malaysia could become so industrialised that it will not need to import manufactured goods from Japan and Australia.

This is, of course, only an example. It may be just a pipe dream on the part of Malaysians like me. But dreams should not be dismissed simply because they seem far-fetched at the moment. Now if this example is multiplied by six, with different commodities of course, the volume of trade between the Asean countries and Australia and Japan could be greatly increased—and, of course, would be better balanced.

Another approach would be to make the Asean countries a halfway house where intermediate processes are carried out. Australian iron ore is at the moment processed in a sintering plant in the Philippines and then shipped to Japan. Singapore refines crude oil from the Middle East for many countries in this region. This is something that can be repeated many times with numerous raw materials coming from Australia destined for Japan and other countries. If we consider how rich in energy and labour some of the Asean countries are, it follows that this halfway house intermediate processing can in fact be an approach that will benefit all the three partners. If seems to me that everyone will gain and no one will stand to lose.

A third approach is the relocation of certain industries which are no longer suitable for Japan and Australia. Obviously labour intensive industries should no longer be located in these two countries. They would do better in the Asean countries. Low technology industries where the value added is not high would form another group. Energy intensive industries too come within the category of industries that should be relocated.

In all instances it is worthwhile to remember that Asean countries are among the most stable in the world and they all welcome foreign involvement in their economy. Its good business to do business with them.

If all these fanciful ideas are put into effect and the linkages between Asean, Australia and Japan become a reality, what would be the effect on the trading patterns of with other parts of the world will be affected. But the most likely scenario would be accelerated prosperity of the region which, if the present interest in Southeast Asia is any indication, would result in a rush on the part of developed countries to do business with this group. Indeed, the new prosperity would spill over to the rest of the world. Despite Japan and Australia, there would still be a need to buy sophisticated products from the developed countries and also goods and other products from other developing countries. In other words, extensive economic cooperation between Japan, Australia and Asean, along the lines mentioned earlier, will benefit the economy of the world much the same way as the American economy affects the world. Indeed, the world's economy would not have to depend so much on that of America or of Europe. A new economic dynamo in the West Pacific would be able to take up the slack.

Having indulged in these flights of fancy, let me come down to earth. What in fact is the relation between Asean, Australia and Japan? I have mentioned that Asean is largely a supplier of raw materials to Japan and Australia. Sentiments in both Japan and Australia favour protectionism. This is a strange sentiment considering that both countries are affected by American and European protectionism. One would think that being victims of protectionism, both would sympathise with the Asean countries' infantile steps towards exporting manufactured goods. But the fact is that protectionism is very strong especially in Japan.

If there is to be meaningful economic relations between Australia, Japan and Asean, then protectionism must be reduced or modified. Tariff and non-tariff barriers (NTBs) should be gradually dismantled. Instead there should be positive efforts made to ease the entry of manufactured goods from Asean into both countries. Where manufacturing is done by joint-venture companies involving either Japan or Australia with Asean, buyback arrangements should be encouraged in order to provide ready markets which in turn will support large scale production.

Next comes the problem of shipping. Asean countries must be given a fair share in the carriage of goods between them and Japan and Australia. Earnings from the carriage of freight are very substantial. If we are going to avoid excess shipping tonnage, some form of joint operations of shipping lines should be contrived at. Ships plying between Asean and Japan, and Asean and Australia should be pooled and manned by mixed crews. There will be problems of course, but the shipping industry should learn from airlines how to cooperate when competition is mutually damaging.

Air services should be liberalised. There should be more landing rights and more joint operations. The kind of rigid criteria for landing rights which is normally applied to airlines of developed countries should not be applied to the developing countries of Asean.

The world is getting smaller and more interdependent. There is no way by which we can isolate ourselves, whether we are developed or developing. Since we have to live and depend on each other, the best things to do is to accept the fact and make the best of it.

5

Asean and the Pacific Community

"No one can deny that great strides have been made by all the Asean countries. Such is their achievement that Asean has become the second most effective regional grouping in the world, next to the EEC."

THE presence of so many distinguished participants from Europe and other parts of the world at this gathering must give cause for much satisfaction for the organisers, as it must to the people in this region who are anxious to learn from all

---

A speech delivered at the International Conference on Southeast Asia and the Pacific Age organised by the Association for the Promotion of International Cooperation of Japan and ISIS Malaysia in Kuala Lumpur, Malaysia, on December 3, 1984

continents. At the same time it affords the world an opportunity to know of the problems, hopes and aspirations of the people of this region. No country or community can just be concerned only with the area or region that they are in. Whether we like it or not, we have all become citizens of the world.

Permit me to say a few words about Southeast Asia and the Pacific Age—the theme of your conference. The Pacific is nobody's lake. It is a vast ocean that for centuries divided two of the biggest land masses—Asia and the Americas. For a very long time the peoples of the two continents knew nothing of each other.

But the wonders of modern communication have made the Pacific more of a lake than the Mediterranean was to the conquering Romans. Today aeroplanes crisscross the Pacific in a matter of hours, while voices can be heard and scenes viewed the very instant they happen. And so it is no longer strange to talk of Pacific Rim countries or even to propose a Pacific Community. So far we have not gone beyond the stage of talking. And for a long time we will only talk. But it is a subject worth talking. Imagine a community united by a vast ocean instead of by a continent. It may seem a little far-fetched except that the physical obstacles are no longer there. What remains are political and cultural obstacles. Yet compared to Europe in the first half of this century and before, there are less political obstacles in the path of a Pacific Community. But cultural obstacles remain and they are powerful and for the moment conclusive.

The fact is that the Pacific Rim is peopled by people of differing races and cultures, and different stages of development. Unlike Europe which is relatively homogeneous, even the Asians in the Pacific Rim are different from each other. For a long time they know nothing of each other. Naturally they are prejudicial against each other. Such is their difference that even a minimum programme of cooperation is impossible at the moment. And so for a long time there will be no Pacific Community. But this does not mean there isn't or there will not be a Pacific Age. The fact is that for very different reasons each and every Pacific Community has exhibited vigorous growth in the past twenty years or so. Such is the economic achievement that

they have largely outstripped Europe—the centre of modernisation in the last two or three centuries. The indicators show that their growth is likely to continue even if there is no institutionalised relationship between the countries of the Pacific Rim. It pays, therefore, to recognise such growth and to study the effect on both the countries within and the countries outside the region. It may be just an academic exercise which influences not at all the governments concerned. But such studies may still provide greater understanding of the mechanism, the successes and the mistakes that human societies and communities make. It may provide posterity with a model that they can emulate or avoid as the case may be. In any case, it is far better to make contemporary observation than to have future historians deduce, influenced as they must be by their own contemporary environment and bias.

So much for the Pacific, the Pacific Rim, the Pacific Community and the Pacific Age. But we are interested in Southeast Asia, a component of the Pacific Rim that is reputed to be dynamic and growing in importance every day. It is not quite correct, of course, to say that the whole of Southeast Asia is dynamic, economically speaking. Several countries in the Southeast Asia region are actually stagnating or even regressing. The

Indochinese peninsula is still involved in a debilitating war from which it can only emerge weaker and more subservient to foreign powers. Political ambitions and outdated ideas of racial hegemony have led to the expansion of vast amounts of man, money and material in a futile war of conquest. The immediate effect is to make the ambitious conqueror itself a client state and a vassal of a foreign power. In the long term it will impoverish the whole of the peninsular, once the seat of some of the greatest of ancient Asian civilisation.

Indochina excepted, the rest of Southeast Asia tells a different story. Although there may be temporary setbacks, on the whole the countries of Southeast Asia excluding Indochina are doing extremely well. Politically they are stable, i.e., when compared to the other newly independent countries. Economically they all adhere to a free-market system, where home-grown entrepreneurs have brought about economic growth that is remarkable even by developed world standards. Thus through the 1970s and 1980s while the U.S. and Europe grew by an average 2.9 per cent per annum, the growth for the Asean countries averaged 6 to 8 per cent. In the last decade domestic investments grew by 1.9 per cent per year in the U.S. and 3.1 per cent in Japan. In the Asean countries growth in domestic investment ranged from 7 to 14 per cent.

It may be coincidental but the Asean countries comprising Indonesia, Malaysia, Singapore, Thailand and the Philippines, seem to have done well since the formation of their Association. Yet Asean is far from being an economic community. It was regional politics that prompted the setting up of Asean. Out of the ashes of Confrontation Asean rose like the proverbial phoenix. It should really be an economic animal but, try as the members might, they have not really succeeded in the field of economic cooperation. Instead they have been politically more cohesive, consulting and working with each other not only on regional matters but even when dealing with global affairs. Indeed, their political cohesiveness is one of the most important aspects of Asean.

Even though economic cooperation has not been remarkable, the fact is that the members of Asean have each been economically dynamic. With the admission of Brunei into the membership, the group's combined economic performance must be among the most remarkable in the world today. Even the world economic recession has failed to bring the kind of disasters experienced by other developing countries.

What is the reason behind this performance? Economic cooperation may be minimal, but there is ample evidence that the Asean countries tend to learn from each other. When the open economies of some of the members proved beneficial to economic growth, narrow nationalistic socialism with attendant nationalisations were abandoned. Foreign investment was encouraged, with each country devising a set of incentives in order to attract the highest amount of foreign capital.

Domestically private enterprise began to replace unbearable. Today the process of denationalisation has progressed to a point where privatisation has not only become respectable but has become a by-word in the Association. In Malaysia privatisation has been made possible by the emergence of a group of indigenous entrepreneurs who have benefited from the NEP.

Government expenditure on infrastructure and administrative reforms attracted the attention of all the Asean governments. While there are still a lot of weaknesses there is no doubt that the governments of

Asean countries have become more efficient and outward-looking, at least by comparison to the state of affairs before the emergence of Asean.

No one can deny that great strides have been made by all the Asean countries. Such is their achievement that Asean has become the second most effective regional grouping in the world, next to the EEC.

Perhaps the Asean experience could provide a guide for greater Pan Pacific cooperation. Asean has become a successful and effective grouping not tied together so much by the dictates of contractual obligations and treaty undertakings as by a strong sense of community and what we in Asean call the "Asean spirit". Asean is not premised on any grand design. There is no great economic or political blueprints. But the spirit of partnership continues to be nurtured even as we continue to give priority to each of our national interests. Over the course of time, and because of the broadest range of shared discussions, shared activities and shared decision-making, there has arisen cooperation and partnership for progress, interdependence and a mutuality of interests.

Grand economic designs were disregarded at the inception of Asean. To expect too much would have resulted in achieving nothing. If Asean had started out to become another EEC, it would never have got off the ground. People and nations cannot get on together until they know each other. If there is going to be some quantum leap in cooperation between the countries of the Pacific, then the appalling ignorance even among neighbours in the region must be overcome.

It follows that if the Pacific Rim countries are interested in some form of association, a grand economic design should be the last thing that they should think of. Instead, they should try to get to know each other better. As a start discussions of non-controversial issues of interest to everyone, such as meteorology, rescue operations, charting the seas and oceans and the like could be held. Over the course of time, more and more subjects could be discussed and new areas of cooperation embarked upon. All the time, the numerous contacts, formal and informal, multilateral or bilateral, will stimulate a greater knowledge and appreciation of each other. In time, a sense of community will emerge that will make mutual help and cooperation almost second nature. If in the meantime deliberate programmes of studies and exchanges such as this Global Community Forum are organised, the process can be considerably accelerated.

Today it seems to be fashionable to talk in terms of the Global citizen, the Global Community and things that are Global in nature. While it is a noble concept that ought to be pursued and at the same time a very good academic exercise, nevertheless we should not lose track of the more immediate problems facing us today. While we are gathered here, exchanging ideas and thoughts on how we can work globally, there are many others elsewhere who are working and even scheming to make the world anything but global. I refer to those countries who have now become more inward looking, and are only thinking of their own selfish interest. We see states forming groupings or exclusive clubs to keep others out of their combined markets. World bodies and organisations are ignored. Much work now tends to be done outside the framework of the United Nations. Far from showing greater concern for the developing countries, the advanced North have introduced tariff and non-tariff barriers, to hinder and frustrate the economic advancement of the developing South. The developed countries have also come out with other measures under the guise of assisting domestic industry and stimulating domestic economic growth. In reality, they are nothing but protectionist measures to deprive the entry of products from developing countries.

Of course, the developed countries by virtue of their economic strength and control of the world's economic systems can go on doing this. They can continue to influence the world markets to their advantage. They can continue to deprive the legitimate interests of the South. They can also continue to carve their spheres of economic influence. But these developed nations must surely realise that in the end there will be a price to pay. We are really interdependent and even the developed must one day bow to the developing. We saw the results of the prolonged exploitation of the oil producing countries. Surely we do not want to see that repeated in other areas even if it be on a lower scale.

The inequities in our shrinking world must be reduced and the developed countries cannot dismiss these inequities as irrelevant. The collapse of the financial systems in some developing countries carries a lesson for all. As much as the developing countries must be responsible, the developed countries must also stop shirking their responsibilities.

It is also disheartening to note that there are those who still believe that if you want peace, you must prepare for war and that the only guarantee of stability is the creation of balances of military power. In the past it may have been logical for a peace-loving nation to be so well-armed for defence that no one will dare to attack it. But in these days of enormously expensive star-wars weapons, such a notion is ridiculous. No sooner have you invented a weapon to defend yourself against the latest in weapons of mass destruction when the other side will come up with a weapon to render ineffective your defence system. And the same is true the other way round. The result will be an escalation of expenditure on defence and offence that will pull the rest of the world along with them. We are seeing it happening now. The Global Community which sounds so good may only mean global destruction if the idea of preparing for war in order to avoid it is carried to its logical conclusion.

We, in Malaysia, believe that the first line of defence of any country is not its military capabilities. The first line of defence lies in it's national resilience and in shaping a strategic environment where threats are minimised. It lies in the policy of making friends with those who want to be friends with us. This Global Community Forum I hope will be part of this exercise in making friends.

6

Moderate Achievement in Asean's Economic Cooperation

"Asean is considered the bright spot in the turbulent world of today. Even in a recession we have largely managed to maintain economic growth."

THE foundation of cooperation among the countries of Asean was laid more than a decade ago by the Bangkok Agreement and the Bali Declaration of Asean Concord. Today we can be proud that Asean has made considerable progress as a regional grouping. Internationally, Asean has attained

---

A speech delivered at the 17th Meeting of Asean Economic Ministers (AEM) in Kuala Lumpur, Malaysia, on February 7, 1985

political prominence and credibility. Within the member countries themselves Asean consciousness is palpable. Our political cooperation and common stand on many international issues are expected and accepted by the international community and we have gained considerably by this. It is no coincidence that the member countries of Asean are politically stable and that the region has consistently registered economic growth well above world average.

While Asean has made significant achievements in the fields of political, cultural and social cooperation, in the field of economic and trade cooperation the achievement has been mediocre or worse. I would therefore suggest we now reflect on what has been achieved in this field thus far. Since the historic Bali Summit in 1976, there has been a proliferation of committees; all of which were set-up with the common objective of enhancing Asean's cooperation programmes. Countless meetings have been convened. The Asean Economic Ministers are now meeting for the 17th time. Undoubtedly all the above inputs were aimed at achieving our ideal of increased trade and economic cooperation. The Asean Preferential Trading Arrangement (PTA) now include an impressive list of more than 18,000 items. Other areas of cooperation such as food, science and technology, energy, health, transport and communication have also been laboriously discussed at meetings after meetings. However, the fact remains that trade among Asean countries is still relatively small accounting for only about 20 per cent of Asean's global trade. It is even smaller if the entrepôt trade through Singapore is excluded. Asean's trade covered by the PTA represent only a fraction of total intra-Asean trade. This is indeed an unsatisfactory state of affairs.

I am aware that similarities in our economic structures have to a certain degree made us potential competitors rather than partners. Furthermore, the difference in the economic conditions in our countries rule out any common-market-type arrangements. But there are many areas where we can achieve some degree of complementarity. I believe that we should now seriously examine the areas for common endeavour. We need a new and more serious commitment to developing our economic cooperation.

In order to assist us in intensifying further our cooperative efforts we should try to know each other better. Perhaps we should begin by exchanging more information on trade among ourselves. Research and analysis based on this information could possibly identify the items which we can literally exchange. I am not suggesting barter or countertrade but surely there must be quite a number of items which each one of us needs but which we obtain from outside Asean. Yet there are members of Asean currently producing these items. The volume that we buy from each other can be counterbalanced. That way no one would be the loser, yet total intra-Asean trade would gain. The Asean Secretariat should consider setting up a data bank covering such areas as export and import items in addition to economic indicators, tariffs, tax structures, non-tariff legislations, etc. The Secretariat could play a pivotal role in this regard and should give intra-Asean trade top priority.

It would not be complete to talk of economic cooperation without touching on commodities. Here I would like to define commodities as being not only naturally produced agricultural and mineral products but also undifferentiated manufactured products. This definition is necessary because the developing countries are being persuaded more and more to buy and put up plants which produce manufactured commodities in excessive quantities. The plant fabricators make a lot of money up front while excessive production ensure that the particular commodity floods the market with the expected results.

There is no doubt that commodities will continue to feature as an important component of our economies especially from the view point of contribution to export earnings. In recent years, commodity prices have been adversely affected by structural changes and recessionary conditions in the world economy. As a result commodity producers faced problems of achieving reasonable returns. Indeed, in some instances the more we produce the more we lose. But faced with closure and unemployment and the over whelming need to earn foreign exchange, we have no choice but to continue producing. Our only consolation is that in a recession even the most sophisticated products can suffer the same fate.

While effective worldwide commodity agreements are worth pursuing, intra-Asean cooperation on commodities should not be ignored. The combined production of certain commodities by the Asean countries is such that the voice of Asean carry considerable weight in commodity agreements. I am not suggesting the formation of cartels but there is no reason why we should not use our combined strength to influence our trade. The developed world is doing the same when they talk of market forces. Those forces are located in their countries and are controlled by them. Asean cooperation in commodities would actually be defensive. Divided we will succumb one by one. United we will stand a reasonable chance.

I would like to point out here that although the Japanese, the European and the American governments seem to be fighting each other over trade, their big manufacturers are actually collaborating with each other. Indeed, in a book by Kenichi Ohmae of McKinsey & Company, Inc., the international management consulting firm, which will be published soon, it would appear that the three powerful northern economies have actually divided the international marketplace among themselves with Southeast Asia going to the Japanese, West Asia and Africa to the Europeans and Central and South America to the U.S. How do we fight this if we compete against each other excessively in the international marketplace?

Despite our appeal to the developed consumer countries to work together with the south in the spirit of economic interdependence, it is the efforts of producers themselves which will ultimately determine the fate of our commodities. While the required effort may be too burdensome for any one producer, by grouping together as producers association, we can tackle the problem more effectively. It is for this reason that Malaysia attaches a lot of importance to the establishment and strengthening of producers associations like the ANRPC and ATPC. We are glad that Asean colleagues have in the spirit of solidarity and mutual benefit joined us in this endeavour. Now that we have established these bodies, there is the even more challenging task of ensuring that these bodies and others like them fulfil their objectives.

Turning to the international economic arena, it is evident that the world economy has become increasingly interdependent. This has brought both prosperity and problems for the developing countries, including Asean countries. The developed countries are the main sources not only of machinery and equipment, but also of technology and know-how so essential for the economic progress of the Asean countries. The developed countries are also important for Asean not only in terms of markets for exports, both primary products and manufactures, but also as a source of investment. How ever, the recent global recession has witnessed developed countries resorting to inward-looking, domestically palatable policies, affecting both market access and investment capital. There has emerged, of late, what I would refer to as 'free traders of convenience' who frantically proclaim themselves as the standard bearers of free trade, except in situations which affect them adversely. There has been a spate of increase in protectionist measures by developed countries. Their unilateral protectionist actions as exemplified by recent trade measures and devising criteria to exclude some of our products from GSP benefits, the concept of 'Graduation', countervailing duties, and the more recent stringent trade legislations are all manifestations of the lack of political will of developed countries to honour their commitments to developing countries whose markets and resources they continue to exploit.

An area that we have missed before is the invisible trade. Freight and insurance, travel and education abroad have either negated or worsened our trade balance. The 40:40:20 ratio in freight, for example, has been ignored and we find great difficulty in securing landing rights. We do not believe in cartels and ganging up but if the Asean countries fail to coordinate our approach in dealing with the developed countries, we will never be able to redress the imbalances. There is no need for me to stress the effect of these imbalances on our domestic development.

Asean's economic relations with its dialogue partners constitute an important element of Asean economic cooperation. In fact, the Asean region represents a significant and growing export market for our dialogue partners and is among their fastest growing markets. While Asean's cooperative efforts with third countries and international organisations have led to some progress in certain areas, meaningful results have yet to be achieved in others. In the key area of improved market access for Asean's exports for example, the dialogue partners have not responded positively so far. This is most regrettable and partly may be attributed to Asean's inability to harness its strength and act in concert to enhance our trading interest. Our six Asean nations presently represent a market of well over US$70 billion. This makes our purchasing power about half of Japan's or equal to that of Canada's. The region's population of about 270 million with a progressively increasing per-capita income provides a ready market for all kinds of products and services. Asean's imports grew faster than most other group of countries in the world. The increasing number of trade missions from the developed countries to the Asean region is a reflection of the fact that the centre of gravity of global economic activities is now shifting from the Atlantic to the Pacific. Asean is considered the bright spot in the turbulent world of today. Even in a recession we have largely managed to maintain economic growth. It is time that Asean undertakes a review of her dialogue programmes. Our dialogue partners should be made to realise that it is in their enlightened self-interest to establish a mutually beneficial relationship and take more seriously the dialogue with Asean countries.

In our efforts to promote economic cooperation among Asean countries, we should also harness the vital inputs of our private sectors. Their contributions in translating cooperative ideals into tangible results are imperative. Concerted efforts by the Asean private sectors are essential for undertaking measures to enhance intra-Asean trade. The private sector should act as an important linkage to supplement and complement the efforts of the government in attracting the flow of capital and investment. New efforts must be made by the private sector with the Asean Chambers of Commerce and Industry (ACCI) as the spearhead. They should not be too discouraged by their lack of progress or their frustrations in dealing with six different bureaucracies. The governments for their part should be more accommodating and should put Asean interest in the forefront. The success of Asean will mean the prosperity and well-being of each member country. If we fail to support each other, we will end up making the rich developed countries richer.

That Asean is a tangible and successful grouping of nations is acknowledged by all. As is usual this success is not welcome by some. Of late there has been oblique attempts to sour relations between Asean countries and, in particular, their leaders.

We have been particularly careful never to publicly criticise each other. We are not perfect and before we throw stones, we usually look at our own glass houses and decide otherwise. This has enabled us to get along with each other. But others are now coming up with dubious quotes which are calculated to sour relations between Asean partners.

We must resist the temptation to react. Outsiders do not have the interest of Asean at heart. Indeed, they would like to destroy it. Whether they succeed or not depends upon us. It we get uptight then we have only ourselves to blame.

7

Asean: Challenges and Opportunities

"It is time for those of us who believe dearly in Asean, who see vast potential for economic cooperation, to stop being merely dreamers and to be doers. It is time for us who recognise the great opportunities to stop waiting and to start moving."

WE meet at a time of challenge and a time of opportunity. The challenges must be confronted by creative dexterity and iron resolve, with pragmatism guided by a clear strategic vision with regard to the dictates of our national interest and the demands of Asean's future development. The

---

A speech delivered at the 18th Asean Ministerial Meeting in Kuala Lumpur, Malaysia, on July 8, 1985

opportunities must be grasped with equal creativity, with equal resolve, with a pragmatism that is similar and guided by the same depth of strategic vision.

For a long time, to echo a phrase, "we never had it so good." To be sure, the 1970s was a period of international economic turmoil; but it was also a period of economic opportunity. Many countries in other parts of the world did badly. Many others did even worse. We in Asean performed exceedingly well, generally emerging as the fastest growing region in the world. Economic historians will say that we were not part of the passenger carriages being pulled. We were part of the engine of growth of the entire Pacific Basin and of the global economic system.

We still are part of the engine of growth and the days ahead are by no means dark. But the skies in the rest of the 1980s threaten much rain and many storms. The prospects for commodity prices in the short and medium term demand that we continue to strengthen our efficiency as world beaters. The productivity push must be taken to new heights. The tide of growing protectionism and more blatant commodity market manipulation demand that we act with resolve and where necessary in concert to keep the open doors from being closed and to break the stranglehold of institutions created by marketeers for themselves. We appreciate all that is being done in Japan and the U.S. and elsewhere by those who believe in open doors. We strongly deprecate the actions of those who champion protectionism.

In a fast-changing international environment, we must continue to be quick of foot, able to respond at the governmental level and in the private sector to market changes and product demands. We must make sure that the economic tensions between our friends—the U.S.

and Japan—are not escalated, indeed that they are dissipated. Above all we must ensure that the solution of their problem should not be at our expense. Then of course we must continue to find the means by which economic cooperation within Asean can be taken in new directions and to new levels. Malaysia, together with the other states of Asean, must continue to ensure that Asean remains the focus of our attention and the cornerstone of our foreign policy.

The biggest political challenge confronting Asean today, as in the recent past, is the Kampuchean question. Unfortunately, of late there has been a lack of response to the initiatives of Asean. We must continue to exercise patience. At the same time, we must continue to be proactive, to consider every possibility, and to work with determination and creativity in our tireless search for a just, productive, and viable political solution, a solution that will be just, productive and viable in the long term as well as in the short run.

It is Malaysia's view that for such a just, productive and viable solution the following imperatives will have to be met. Firstly, the suffering of the Kampuchean people must be ended while Thailand's security must be ensured. This is basic. Then there must be a government of national reconciliation, and the Kampuchean people must be provided with the opportunity to exercise their right of self-determination and to ensure a state of Kampuchea that is sovereign and independent. This obviously means that finally foreign troops cannot be on Kampuchean soil.

The only guarantee of a viable solution to the Kampuchean problem lies in the reasonable accommodation of the vital interests of all the parties to the dispute, in creating a situation that all can live with and none will set about to undo. Those who neglect the lessons of history may be condemned to repeating it. Let us not forget Geneva. Let us not forget that true peace, true stability, true security are dynamic processes, which have to be sustained over time. As much as the other states in the Indochinese peninsula and indeed everywhere else desire to live free and independent in their own homeland, so do the Kampuchean people.

For a settlement to be productive in terms of the long-term peace, security and stability of Southeast Asia, it is essential that we understand that our concern must not only be with the short run but also the longer-term future of the region. We should aspire to a solution that is provocative of no Power. We should aspire to a political solution which establishes the ground rules for the game of peace in Southeast Asia, which establishes the principle that there must be respect for each other's independence and territorial integrity, which establishes the principle of non-interference in each other's internal affairs, and which establishes the principle of pacific settlement—the living rule that all disputes shall be resolved by peaceful means. We should also aspire to a solution that will enhance the prospects for the realisation of our common goal for a Zone of Peace, Freedom, and Neutrality in this region, where confidence and understanding can flourish and cooperation can prosper.

Such a just, productive and viable solution is, unfortunately not at hand. We in Asean must therefore continue to strive to bring it about. Clearly Vietnam must be brought to realise the need to engage in meaningful dialogues with us and with the parties concerned so as to remove the impediments to peace in Kampuchea. It is time for Vietnam to respond constructively to the Asean approaches.

If the Kampuchean problem poses the biggest political challenge to our ingenuity, our creativity and our efforts, the problem of *dadah* or drug abuse and illicit trafficking poses the biggest social challenge. In your countries as in mine, we have undertaken great efforts to deal with this dreaded disease. We have sought to move our nations, to galvanise our society in the war against narcotics. It is time to take the fight to the international arena and to create a world concert against the abuse of drugs and the criminals who perpetrate this crime against humanity. In this context, Malaysia welcomes the timely call of the Secretary-General of the United Nations for the convening of a World Conference of Ministers to initiate a programme of concrete action. I would go further. Given the gravity of the situation and the universality of this grave menace to mankind, is there not a need to push most vigorously for a United Nations organisation similar to the organisation for refugees? I call upon you to impress upon all the Asean dialogue partners the necessity and the urgency of a concerted global war against a menace that recognises no boundaries and that threatens all societies in every part of the world.

I have mentioned what to me are the most serious economic, political and social challenges to Asean and to Asean's ingenuity and energies. Let me now dwell a little on the opportunities that Asean offers.

It might be argued that in the more uncertain economic situation that will confront us in the days ahead, the opportunity to take Asean economic cooperation to new frontiers will be more complicated. If anything, now is not the most opportune time. There may be some veracity in this. But let us ask ourselves: how often in the life of an organisation, as in the life of a man, does the 'most opportune time' come? When, in the life of Asean, will the most opportune time for economic cooperation arrive? Do we merely sit and wait? Or do we move to create the conditions and to mould the events that will allow us to achieve the breakthroughs we must have with regard to economic cooperation?

We have heard the saying that nothing is more powerful than an idea whose time has come. I am one who believes that it must be one of the fundamental tasks of true leadership to take a powerful idea and to make its time come. The opportune time, like good luck, may happen by chance. But it more often comes about by the sweat of our brows and by the courage of our convictions, by human effort allied to human determination. It is time for those of us who believe dearly in Asean, who see vast potential for economic cooperation, to stop being merely dreamers and to be doers. It is time for us who recognise the great opportunities to stop waiting and to start moving.

We now see our entrepreneurs and traders eyeing the 'vast' China market, but missing or dismissing the reality that is before their very eyes: the Asean market. Statistics tell us what our deflected imaginations fail to grasp: that the Asean market is four times the size of the China market. That the Asean market is at our very doorstep, not in a faraway land whose business practices and systems are uncertain, and in some areas, still an unknown quantity. We now see some of our investors eyeing China as an attractive place for their investment, when vast opportunities exist in Asean in every area of business activity.

There are, no doubt, various obstacles to greater economic cooperation within Asean. But to the negative thinkers, let me pose this question: in what worthwhile human endeavour do we not encounter serious obstacles? To be sure, the economies of the Asean countries are generally competitive rather than complementary. But can we not seek the many areas of complementarity, which are there in even the most complementary system, and exploit them to our mutual advantage? Is it not time for our private sector to know as much about the markets of each of the Asean states as we know about the markets of Japan, of Europe and of the U.S.?

Let not my remarks be misunderstood. Asean has been a resounding success. Even if we make little headway in the area of economic cooperation, Asean will continue to remain a vital institution. It will remain a vigorous and productive endeavour. If Asean did not exist, we would have had to invent it. But this year as in years past we have an opportunity, indeed, an obligation to all our peoples not only to consolidate Asean, but also to strive to break new ground, to take each new challenge and to turn it into a new opportunity.

8

Asean's Focus in the Early Years Was Political

"But the decision to cooperate politically and to resolve problems among neighbours through negotiation is not totally without economic benefits. None of the Asean countries would have developed economically if their political wranglings could not be resolved."

YOU will agree with me that in its first twenty years the main thrust of Asean has been political. This is as it should be and we have no need for regrets. We should remember that it was political problems between us as neighbours that first brought us together. If I may say so, we have been kept separate by our former colonial masters (except for Thailand) so

A speech delivered at the 1st Asean Economic Congress in Kuala Lumpur, Malaysia, on March 13, 1987

much so that we really knew nothing of each other and were only too ready to mistrust one another. But the resulting political problems forced us to negotiate and eventually to appreciate the futility of Confrontation. We then formed the ASA and eventually Asean.

But when Asean was formed, the EEC was in its early idealistic years. Invariably, a lot of people, particularly outsiders, saw in Asean a mirror image of the EEC—an economic community. They dismissed the importance of regional political cooperation and began talking of common markets. Foreign investors and traders saw Asean as a huge market, access to which can be gained through one or two countries they think they could handle.

The reality is that we are separate nations with the interest of our own people at heart. We were not about to discard our newfound nationalism in favour of unclear regional loyalties. Although some of us were enamoured of the common market idea, most found themselves quite unable to dismantle policies and systems based on nationalism. After all the EEC then and even now is not such a resounding success.

But the decision to cooperate politically and to resolve problems among neighbours through negotiation is not totally without economic benefits. None of the Asean countries would have developed economically if their political wranglings could not be resolved. Imagine what would happen to the economies of Malaysia and Indonesia if the Confrontation had continued and escalated. Imagine the money that would be lost, the tensions and the poor investment climate that would result if the Philippines' claim to Sabah had resulted in a face-off between Malaysia and the Philippines.

The decision to cooperate politically not only marked the maturity of the early Asean leaders but quite definitely laid the foundation for economic developments of the members. Although we do compete, we also learnt a lot from each other about how to manage a developing country with a market economy and dependent largely on the export of commodities. Such was the success of the Asean countries economically that together they became a show-piece of regional cooperation and development. It is a truism to say that no other regional grouping has done as well economically, and of course politically, as Asean.

But we mustn't pat our backs too much. We have done well but we must realise that in the modern world's economy those who don't move forward will soon find themselves left very far behind. We have to run merely to maintain our position in the economic pecking order.

The economy of the world has changed tremendously since Asean was formed. For us the most telling of these changes is the collapse of commodity prices and the forced depreciation of our national currencies. As a result we are not only earning less from our commodity exports but we have to pay more for necessary manufactured goods as well as to service our debts.

It is axiomatic that one person's loss is another person's gain. The losses suffered by the commodity producers like Asean and the OPEC countries meant definite gains by the developed countries. Indeed, it is estimated that the developed countries received a gift of something like US$100 billion from the poor developing countries in 1986 alone. Consequently their economy has grown by about 3 per cent, which is extremely high by the standards of developed countries.

But that is not all. A protectionist trend has developed directed largely at Japan. Unfortunately, many developing countries are caught by protectionist laws and will suffer losses in export earnings.

In addition trade in goods has given way to trading in currencies and shares. There is more fast money to be made in buying and selling of money and shares than in the manufacture and sale of goods. Raw materials are not involved in this kind of business and again the developing countries will lose out.

In the face of all these radical changes, what do we do? Commodities may recover, as indeed some have, but they will never be as valuable as export earners as before. We may take the route taken by the Newly Industrialised Countries (NICs)—South Korea, Taiwan and Hong Kong—i.e., we manufacture goods for exports. They are extremely well-off now. We may also take advantage of the expensive Yen—and become the manufacturing centres for Japanese enterprises which can no longer manufacture economically in Japan.

All these routes are worth trying and will no doubt help our economies. The danger is that when our exports of manufactured goods go up we may be forced to revalue our currencies as Japan has been forced to.

What else is there left for us to do? As a regional grouping we must try to find some economic advantage from working together. There is really no need to give up our national aspirations completely. But we must realise that truly "National Products" are now passe. Most manufactured goods are now assembled from components made in many different countries. Even Japanese products are not wholly manufactured in Japan. With the rising Yen the foreign contents are going to increase. "Made in Japan" may soon mean only assembled in Japan. In fact, the only thing Japanese about Japanese goods may even be the involvement of Japanese companies in sourcing the components worldwide and assembling them in factories located in the countries where the goods are to be sold.

With the expansion in science and technology no one country can hope to do everything itself. Even the most technologically advanced countries possessing the biggest market must buy certain manufactured items from other countries. No one can surpass the U.S. in making sophisticated commercial aircrafts but Americans must import electronic goods and appliances. Without governments determining policies a kind of division of labour has taken place in the manufacturing world. That division must extend to the developing world—which must be allowed to manufacture the kind of goods they are most likely to be efficient at.

We must not therefore be too concerned about or take too much pride in "National Products." Nor should we try to manufacture everything ourselves. If we want to sell, we must also be prepared to buy. International trade is not a one-way thing. In a regional grouping, the only way to extract economic benefit is to give and take, or sell and buy or in one word, cooperate.

The survival and prosperity of Asean depend on the willingness of member countries to cooperate beyond current individual economic considerations. The need for greater regional cooperation must be considered at par with those related to national development so long as they do not have adverse implications. But Asean must give priority to regional considerations. Intra-Asean trade, for instance, must be radically improved and the current PTA, which now has a staggering 18,000 items, should include items that give substance and meaning to the concept of preferential trading.

There is, I presume, a consensus on the need to enhance intra-Asean trade. the logical follow-up is to enlarge the opportunities for trade. Asean as a group has a common stand in efforts to enlarge its market share in the developed countries of our dialogue partners. Similarly, Asean could create the opportunity for greater intra-Asean trade by opening its market for products from member countries. Perhaps it is time for Asean member countries to state what each is willing to do to create the opportunity. While understandably, national interest will have to be safeguarded, it should be tempered with the realisation that regional gains also contribute towards national growth.

Asean countries must take the initiative to establish a closer, more constructive and complementary relationship. They must not wait too long to assess and decide on necessary adjustments in facing the international economic situation. Substantive steps must be taken in regional cooperation and improvements must be made to the existing framework of intra-Asean cooperation. While Asean hopes for the best possible future, it must prepare for the continuing deterioration of international economic conditions and the obstacles and challenges ahead.

9

Asean Economic Cooperation Needs to be Intensified

"There are no doubt people who understand the nuances and methods upon which Asean cooperation is built. However, there are also those who refuse to acknowledge that despite its shortcomings, Asean has had many achievements which can easily surpass those of other regional groupings."

TWENTY years ago five countries in Southeast Asia came together to establish Asean. Nearly four years ago Brunei joined the ranks of those countries. Now, the strong commitment of the six countries towards Asean has been and will continue to be a dynamic and cohesive regional association of

---

A speech delivered at the 3rd Meeting of the Asean Heads of Government in Manila, the Philippines, on December 14, 1987

states. Asean is indeed a reality in the international system.

Within the two decades of its existence Asean has been able to build an image of sober interregional and international responsibility, maturity and commitment to peaceful development. It has provided the necessary environment for strengthening national and regional resilience which are essential to development, peace and stability in Southeast Asia. The incertitude that hung in the air during the signing of the Bangkok Declaration in 1967 gave way to confidence and firm resolve among the member countries to enhance regional cooperation as enunciated in the Bali Declaration of Asean Concord. That confidence has gained in strength and is again clearly demonstrated here in Manila today. This meeting reaffirms our solidarity and our conviction that Asean remains viable for promoting economic development, social progress and peace and security in the region.

Asean today has brought into sharp focus the vision of its founding Heads of Government, two of whom, I must say with great respect and esteem, are still among us here at this meeting. Asean has shown that regional cooperation founded upon political, economic and cultural cohesion can lead to development and progress. This is vital for regional stability and security. Regional cooperation as manifested by Asean remains the cornerstone of Malaysia's foreign policy.

Since the Meeting of the Asean Heads of Government in Kuala Lumpur ten years ago, several important developments and changes have taken place in the region and elsewhere. These developments have affected the Asean countries both individually and as a group in various ways.

These developments and changes present both formidable challenges and vast opportunities. I believe Asean should and could respond to those challenges squarely. We do not lack the resources. We have the combined potential of more than 250 million people whose creativity and innovative ability are considerable. Given this invaluable asset, it remains only for us to match it with the varied and rapid advances in science and technology to turn the region into a powerhouse of economic and social advancement.

The Asean countries have the natural resources and productive capacity to venture into many areas of economic activity in order to realise the region's full potential and to truly turn Asean into a growth centre for the future. Rightly, there should be no unnecessary barriers to our pursuit of economic cooperation. We must have the political will. For as long as we are clear about those objectives, our will should not wane.

Among the great many changes that we in Southeast Asia have faced in the last decade is the prolonged Vietnamese occupation of Kampuchea. There has also been a new correlation in the strategic interests and military presence of the superpowers in the region. These have presented an unfavourable situation for peace and stability in the region.

Asean has channelled a lot of its energies into finding a comprehensive durable solution to the Kampuchean problem. Our efforts should never become less than what they have been. Efforts to find a solution to this problem should not aim only at ensuring total Vietnamese withdrawal and the restoration of the independent, neutral and non-aligned status of Kampuchea, but they should also aim at ending once and for all the rivalry between the major powers in the region so that durable peace, understanding and cooperation could, in the long term, prevail for the whole of Southeast Asia. Let Southeast Asia be for Southeast Asians and let the people of this region get on with the job of maintaining peace and stability for the sake of their own development and progress.

Asean's commitment to the Zone of Peace, Freedom and Neutrality in Southeast Asia (ZOPFAN), as the ultimate goal for a peaceful and stable Southeast Asia should be stronger now in the light of these changes. It is imperative that further efforts be made to effect the early realisation of ZOPFAN. Malaysia, on her part, places great importance on ZOPFAN. We recognise the roles of the major powers, their legitimate interests and their positive contributions in the region. The legitimate interests and positive contributions of the major powers could be enhanced if Southeast Asia remained free from intraregional conflict and major power rivalry.

For us in Southeast Asia, given the region's history, the successful containment of internal threats to our security remains crucial to our development. Each of our countries face different sets of internal security problems. Asean cooperation in the economic areas could positively contribute towards enhancing our national security.

Nevertheless, there are problems affecting security that are common to us all. Drug abuse and illicit trafficking is recognised by us as a menace which needs the concerted efforts of the international community to eradicate. The pernicious effects of this menace need not be recounted. Asean's resolve on this matter has been an example to all countries in countering this terrible scourge faced by mankind. We must remain steadfast in the fight against the drug menace.

For more than a decade the Asean countries have been faced with the problem of Indochinese refugees seeking temporary asylum within our borders, pending resettlement elsewhere. Problems such as this unnecessarily complicates our priorities and distract our attention from the more fundamental objectives of regional development and peace and security. Efforts should be continued to find a durable and effective solution, in particular by solving it at the source. Vietnam and Laos should cooperate in this regard.

Asean has been quite successful in facing the security challenges posed by developments in the region. Our faith in the importance of economic development and social progress as the foundation for peace and security has paid off. Consequently we reject the possibility of Asean evolving into a regional collective security arrangement or military alliance. We are able to do this because of our belief that to win friends one should not create enemies. Our major concern, rightly, has been and should continue to be the promotion of Asean economic cooperation.

The economic challenges being faced by Asean are enormous. Asean has been highly dependent on the world market for the sale of primary commodities and a limited range of manufactured products. Since the early 1970s there has been a relatively small though steady increase in intra-Asean trade. But intra-Asean trade still forms a small proportion of the total Asean trade. Therefore, in the circumstances, Asean's dependence on external markets will continue, making it more important for Asean to be assured of ready access to those markets.

The prolonged imbalances in world trade and increase protectionist trends which are becoming pervasive in the international trading environment do not bode well for Asean. The U.S. continues to incur huge trade deficits and would need to restructure to reverse the trend and maintain a balance. The U.S. still provides the largest market for Asean. Japan's mounting surplus, which has now firmly established her as the world's largest creditor nation, will not be any good to Asean if there are insufficient sustained efforts on Japan's part to liberalise her trading practices and help redress the international trade and monetary situations. The huge debt burden of the developing countries remains a source of instability in the international economic system. The Asean countries, being no exception, have been hurt in varying degrees by the spiralling appreciation of major currencies and the unstable exchange rates.

We are still far from being out of the woods in respect of the problems of low prices and depressed markets for the world's major commodities. The commodity producing countries in Asean have suffered the ill-effects of poor demand, low returns and increasing protectionism in the area of commodities. We face dangerous trends in the developed countries in the form of subsidised agricultural exports, concessional sales and smear campaigns to discredit our products. Asean should increase its efforts in safeguarding its long-term interests in the area of commodities. There is now an urgent need for Asean to give special emphasis to commodity issues by reviewing and restructuring the Asean machinery to accommodate the commodity sector.

The list of economic woes affecting practically all countries in the world is long. Calls for restructuring, increased aid, standstill and rollback on non-tariff barriers have been repeatedly made. Various pledges, resolutions and promises have been uttered, articulated and documented. Yet, while we progress towards the threshold of a new millennium, many of the solutions to the problems at hand remain elusive. We may indeed be in danger of coming close to a serious breakdown in the system if present trends persist. Not only have the gaps in income and standard of living between the North and the South remained wide, there has also been very little narrowing of the chasm that divides the perceptions and views of both sides.

Asean, as a respected regional organisation, should be capable of contributing towards finding some of the solutions through the intensification of economic cooperation among the member countries, through the dialogue process with the dialogue partners and through active participation in the relevant international fora. Asean countries can collectively venture into various areas in order to help themselves as well as to contribute towards a more stable and manageable world economic environment. Increased cooperation among the countries in the South could provide new opportunities for Asean.

Asean has had its share of critics. As leaders of the respective member countries, we have on numerous occasions launched into self-appraisals of Asean which quite inevitably conclude in our own grim, uncomplimentary and critical assessments of Asean's performance in the area of economic cooperation. But let the critics be reminded that while certain specific programmes in Asean economic cooperation may have run into some problems, Asean has succeeded in many other areas. Asean functional cooperation which encompasses a wide range of issues and activities has indeed enhanced the Asean identity. It has certainly increased the awareness and consciousness of Asean among the peoples of our countries, and has allowed them to participate actively in many of Asean's activities. Asean should always be willing to improve, accept new ideas and begin with fresh initiatives to raise the level of cooperation not only among the member countries but also between Asean and the rest of the world.

This Meeting of Heads of Government gives us the opportunity to assess Asean's achievements and look into the new initiatives that have been carefully worked out over the last few months. I am confident that all of us share the view that Asean economic cooperation needs to be intensified. Therefore, we should provide the necessary direction for the future.

One of the areas which could be seriously considered is the encouragement of wider participation of the private sector in the activities of Asean. In this context, I personally feel encouraged that the private sector had taken a keen and active interest in the preparations for this Meeting. I wish to compliment the Group of 14 for its efforts. The Group's contribution has helped to augment the preparatory work carried out by the Ministers and Officials.

A lot of attention has been focussed on this Meeting ever since the decision to hold it was made. I believe there are many supporters and critics—established and potential—who are watching with keen anticipation for the final outcome of this Meeting. There are no doubt people who understand the nuances and methods upon which Asean cooperation is built. However, there are also those who refuse to acknowledge that despite its shortcomings, Asean has had many achievements which can easily surpass those of other regional groupings. The path followed by Asean has certainly shown that a strong commitment to the values of freedom and independence, and respect for individual entrepreneurship and dexterity bring many benefits to the member countries. In sharp contrast, strict adherence to narrow ideologically-based objectives preferred by others have clearly shown many signs of failure.

10

Asean-Japan Cooperation Beneficial

"It is in the interest of Japan and other developed countries to help Asean succeed in its industrialisation programme. Even the short spell of prosperity Asean enjoyed in the 1960s and 1970s has proven beneficial to Japan and other developed countries."

WE consider it an honour that His Excellency Mr Noboru Takeshita finds it appropriate to meet with us from the Asean region in his first overseas trip as the new Prime Minister of Japan. This I believe is an indication of the importance the government of Japan places on its relations with Asean. It further

---

A statement delivered at the Asean Heads of Government Meeting with Japanese Prime Minister Mr Noboru Takeshita in Manila, the Philippines, on December 15, 1987

reflects the strength of Japan's commitment and belief in the future prospects of Asean. We in Asean welcome the gesture as it will contribute to our efforts to maintain, enhance and further consolidate the bond of friendship and cooperation between Asean and Japan.

Asean-Japan partnership, if I may say so, could definitely solve some if not most of our regional economic problems. More than that, it could pave the way to resolving many international economic issues related to debt burden, financial market instability and protectionism. Asean-Japan cooperation covers all economic and political elements which could also be found in other cooperative relationship between developed and developing countries. To our mind, Asean-Japan cooperation could serve as a model for cooperative relationship between the developed countries of the North and the developing countries or group of countries in the South. We hope that these relations would move away from the donor-recipient stereotype to a truly cooperative spirit that would be mutually beneficial and in conditions that both could be proud of.

On behalf of my Asean colleagues, I would like to express our appreciation to Japan and to your excellency personally, for the initiative taken by Japan to allocate a sum of not less than US$2 billion to Asean for the development of our private sector. This gesture on Japan's part is a demonstration of Japan's desire to assist in Asean's economic development. We are pleased that Japan will take into account Asean's wishes in formulating the framework of this new Asean-Japan Development Fund. Asean's stand is that as a new initiative, the fund has to be over and above the existing development assistance programmes extended by Japan to Asean, on terms and conditions that are meaningful and concessional. In addition, the fund must be equitably accessible to all Asean countries and its loans should be untied. We also hope that the fund will include a mechanism to insure Asean countries against the risks of further appreciation of the Yen and that there will be significant efforts to promote market access in Japan for Asean products.

The next step is for Asean and Japanese officials to work out the implementation details of the Fund. Asean will readily submit viable projects for funding. I hope that with the close working relationships which have developed between our officials, the Asean-Japan Development Fund will soon become a reality for the Asean countries.

It cannot be denied that Japan has played a major role in contributing towards industrial development of most Asean member countries. However, much as we appreciate Japan's contribution, we are concerned that more and more Japanese investments are shifting away from this region to the U.S., EEC and China. On behalf of my Asean friends here, we would like to urge the government of Japan to actively encourage its private sector to invest their surplus capital in Asean. Asean has just reached another milestone in its economic cooperation with the just concluded Meeting of the Asean Heads of Government. New measures have been announced in the area of industrial cooperation in pursuing Asean's long-term economic objectives.

The Asean Industrial Joint-Venture (AIJV) scheme in which Japanese private investors have shown very keen interest has been greatly improved, and we hope Japanese businessmen will take advantage of this improved scheme to invest in Asean. Asean with its various and varied resources, its liberal investment policies and attractive investment incentives offers great opportunities for Japanese businessmen. We hope that the Japanese government would further encourage its small- and medium-sized firms to invest in Asean by relocating their industries and encouraging effective transfer of their technology. At the same time, we in Asean would like to see the government of Japan introduce measures that would allow for buyback arrangements of products manufactured by Japanese concerns in Asean. Mr Prime Minister, this arrangement would be the single-most important contribution Japan could make, aimed at realising the objectives of the Asean-Japan Development Fund.

We are all concerned with the political stability and security of our region. With these in mind we have proposed the Zone of Peace, Freedom and Neutrality (ZOPFAN) and more recently, the Nuclear Weapons Free Zone. Our emphasis has always been on the need to build up regional resilience through national resilience. In this regard we have repeatedly urged outside powers to refrain from using countries in this region for political experiments to test their ideological theories. Let us proceed with our preoccupations in bringing economic development and social progress to our people. If at all outside powers have a role, it is in this sphere. The financial and human cost in assisting us in this area is certainly less. It is more acceptable to their domestic constituency if compared to the high expenses in any military venture. Theirs as well as our interest in maintaining political and economic stability in the region can be secured without bloodshed and expensive weaponry.

Asean-Japan type of cooperation on Kampuchea in the interest of a durable peace and stability in the region should be extended to the fields of trade, finance and investment. It would be a pity if the understanding achieved in the political field is not utilised for the equally important economic field.

Looking at the current political economic situation in the Pacific region, you will agree with me that Asean is the brightest spot with the greatest potential for rapid growth. If the 21st century is to be the century of the Pacific, as some have predicted, then cooperation among Pacific countries, particularly Japan and the Asean countries is imperative. Japan's technology and management skills can combine profitably with Asean's vast resources in men and material to contribute fully to the strength of the Pacific. Asean can then develop into a strong economic entity which can contribute to the growth of world trade. It can become one of the affluent markets of the world. Japan and other Pacific Rim countries and indeed the world cannot but benefit from Asean prosperity. It is in the interest of Japan and other developed countries to help Asean succeed in its industrialisation programme. Even the short spell of prosperity Asean enjoyed in the 1960s and 1970s has proven beneficial to Japan and other developed countries.

Japan is physically very close to the Asean countries. Such closeness must result in mutual interchanges not only in trade but also in culture. There could also be more exchange of visits not only by officials, but also by the people as a whole. The recent rise in the value of the yen may inhibit Asean travellers going to Japan, but the very same rise should facilitate Japanese travel to Asean countries. The contacts that will result from such travel will help increase our knowledge of each other and our cooperation.

As we approach the year 2000, it is our hope that Japan will initiate changes in its policies that will effectively bring about an enhanced political, socioeconomic, and cultural role in not only the Southeast Asian region but also in the global context. Such an enhanced role should be achieved before the turn of this century. Asean is confident that Japan would be able to maintain and sustain this role given the tremendous economic and monetary resources that have been building up in Japan since the 1970s. Japan needs to play a positive role commensurate with the trade surplus position that she has achieved. Our expectation is that Japan will conduct itself with the kind of sensitivity that it has shown since the end of the war.

I have been rather frank and forthright in stating Asean's expectations. I trust that Asean-Japan relations is such that frankness is acceptable. The necessity for urgent corrective action and extraordinary efforts cannot be overstated. The world is going through one of the most critical periods in its history and it needs courage and understanding on the part of everyone if we are going to regain equilibrium and restore prosperity.

11

Asean Parliamentarians Has Role in Promoting Democracy

"That the Asean countries have succeeded in mastering the intricacies of democracy and to develop rapidly at the same time is a matter for much satisfaction. We should not gloat over our successes, nor should we rest satisfied with them. There is much to be done still to develop our countries."

THE 3rd Meeting of the Asean Heads of Government took place in Manila in December 1987. The Meeting was a clear manifestation of the depth of regional solidarity and unity that has emerged within Asean. A new impetus was given to the Asean cooperative endeavours to see it through the

---

A speech delivered at the 9th Assembly of the Asean Inter-Parliamentary Organisation (AIPO) in Kuala Lumpur, Malaysia, on January 26, 1988

next decade and beyond. The Asean Heads of Government agreed on a comprehensive Programme of Action aimed at enhancing and upgrading every sector of Asean's multifarious development activities. The Programme of Action is therefore Asean's strategy to meet future challenges in a comprehensive, coordinated and pragmatic way.

The political, economic and social interests of Asean member countries, though diverse, are inextricably intertwined. The increasing strategic and economic importance of Asean and Southeast Asia in general, and the continuing uncertainty in Indochina makes it more imperative for the Southeast Asian region to accelerate development and progress and to maintain durable peace and stability.

The problems of occupied Kampuchea continue to be a source of great concern to us. We in Asean must, however, persevere in the search for a comprehensive political solution without sacrificing the principles of national sovereignty and the right of self-determination of the Kampuchean people. The unsettled situation in Kampuchea indeed represents an impediment to the realisation of the Zone of Peace, Freedom and Neutrality (ZOPFAN) in the region.

Asean's reaffirmation of its commitment to the early realisation of the Zone of Peace, Freedom and Neutrality should be translated into positive action, now that the superpowers themselves have come to a new and positive phase in their relationship. The concept of a Southeast Asian Nuclear Weapon Free Zone is therefore Asean's contribution to the international efforts to keep this region free of nuclear weapons and hence help create a more stable political environment conducive to world peace.

Southeast Asia remains an area of strategic importance in the emerging era of the Pacific in which the major powers would no doubt continue to have a significant role in determining the region's future directions. However, it is the primary responsibility of the nations of the region to ensure a conflict-free Southeast Asia through closer cooperation in the political, economic, social and cultural fields among themselves, as well as with other interested parties.

Significant changes have taken place in the economies of the Asean countries. Asean countries are dependent on external markets for the export of their commodities and increasingly on their manufactured goods. However, the unfavourable global trading conditions, compounded by the protectionist trends in the developed countries have created difficulties for all developing countries, including Asean. With this unhealthy environment it is even more necessary that Asean achieve greater intra-Asean cooperation in industry and trade so as to be less dependent on markets outside our control.

In this scheme of things therefore, where do Parliamentarians stand and how do they contribute towards achieving these goals? While it is the Executive's responsibility to come up with suggestions on policies and their *modus operandi*, the Parliamentarians are equally responsible to find ways to overcome our national and regional problems. Parliamentarians are particularly well-placed to reject legislative measures which will reduce intraregional and world trade.

While the 3rd Asean Summit was taking place, President Ronald Reagan and General Secretary Mikhail Gorbachev, had their summit in Washington. The Treaty they signed to eliminate intermediate and short range nuclear missiles marks an important step in the reduction of nuclear arms and disarmament. It could pave the way for a general multilateral disarmament and usher a new era of understanding among countries of varying shades of political conviction. If this is achieved then developing countries can divert scarce funds from the purchase of arms to the improvement of the living standards of the people.

In recent weeks the problem of the Palestinian refugees has taken new dimensions. In defiance of world opinion and United Nations resolutions, the Tel Aviv regime is continuing its relentless policies of systematic and brutal repression against innocent and unarmed Palestinians in the occupied territories. The increasing atrocities, bloodshed and injustice being inflicted by Israel are against human decency and all that it stands for. Malaysia strongly and emphatically condemns the Tel Aviv regime for its cruelties against Palestinians in the occupied territories, and calls on it to immediately abide by international norms and practice. Israel must respect the inalienable right of Palestinians to a national homeland so that permanent peace and stability could be achieved in West Asia. I would like to suggest that you deliberate on this issue and make appropriate recommendations.

This Assembly is the right forum to discuss the fate of suffering humanity, particularly that of the blacks in South Africa. Malaysia has been unequivocal in the abhorrence and condemnation of the racist white regime in South Africa. We in Malaysia feel strongly that South Africa should be completely ostracised. The excuse that this would hurt the blacks more than the whites have been disproved by the realities we see today. Even without sanctions the blacks are still being oppressed, ill-treated and murdered. The only answer would be for total sanctions and isolation of the racist regime of South Africa.

I would also like to touch on a matter of great importance which has become a serious problem affecting many countries in the world. I refer of course to the scourge of drug addiction which has debilitating effects on the economic and social development of our countries. The International Conference on Drug Abuse and Illicit Trafficking (ICDAIT) has recommended a comprehensive programme for all countries which can go a long way towards ridding ourselves of this scourge. It remains for the countries to implement them. Malaysia is totally committed to the fight. As you know the penalty for trafficking in drugs in Malaysia is death. Since we have demonstrated that we discriminate in favour of no one where Malaysian laws are concerned, Malaysia has become less of a transit country.

We have come a long way in Asean. The forging of a common stand and collective will on matters of vital concern to Asean, both within our region and at the international level, are only the outward signs of the quiet progress we have made in building cohesion and cooperation among our countries. The going has not been entirely smooth. The challenges that have emerged from time to time have tested our collective will as well as the resilience within our countries and in the region as a whole. The success we have had reflects the high priority that each one country has placed on Asean and its viability. As Parliamentarians you have a high duty to entrench this priority and progress.

Asean's solidarity and achievements have had the continuing attention and efforts of our Foreign and Economic Ministers, but we also owe a great deal to the roots of understanding, goodwill and cooperation that have been put down by other governmental, non-governmental and people's institutions across Asean. The Asean Inter-Parliamentary Organisation (AIPO), as the forum of Asean Parliamentarians, has also played its part in developing common framework of approaches and actions on matters of deep concern to all of us. AIPO's contacts with Parliamentarians in Europe, Asia, Australia and elsewhere have been valuable assets.

Indeed, AIPO has provided a unique opportunity for the people of Asean, and our friends from elsewhere, an opportunity to see parliamentary institutions and legislative processes at work in Asean. These reflect our people's will and the diversity of historical and cultural backgrounds that we are heirs to. Democratic and parliamentary institutions and processes have been nurtured and have grown in a meaningful way in the countries of Asean, but they have not escaped the pressures and the tensions created by our cultural, ethnic and religious diversity within each of our countries. They have not yet become totally immunised against the sporadic attacks of adventurous dreamers, of tunnel-visioned proponents of alien concepts and of plain anti-social forces. They will in time become immune, but in the meantime we must manage to hold the fundamentals of our nationhood intact. In the end, democratic and parliamentary processes have to ensure our people the peace and security that they are entitled to.

We in Asean can be proud that we have in fact been able to manage these processes, considering that we have been independent, with the exception of Thailand, only since the end of World War II. Before that we were colonies of Western nations, whose imperial interests preclude training in the art and science of government, particularly the democratic form of government. The colonial governments we were exposed to were, if not totalitarian, at least authoritarian. Except for a few tame nominees, the people of our countries were never represented in these colonial governments.

If these colonial governments had problems, they resolved these problems without any regard for the feelings or interests of the indigenous people. Thus when faced with a shortage of manpower to exploit the resources of their colonies, they did not hesitate to import culturally and ethnically alien people. No effort was made to integrate these people. Indeed, they were deliberately separated in keeping with the dictum 'divide and rule'.

Consequently when independence was gained and democracy was adopted the peoples of these new nations found democracy very difficult to manage. A system does not work merely because it is a good system. What makes it tick is the people who manage or participate in it. Not having had any democratic experience under colonial rule, the peoples of the newly independent countries could not appreciate the restraints and the responsibilities in the exercise of democratic rights.

That the Asean countries have succeeded in mastering the intricacies of democracy and to develop rapidly at the same time is a matter for much satisfaction. We should not gloat over our successes, nor should we rest satisfied with them. There is much to be done still to develop our countries. For this we need stability. Members of Parliament must know this and they must contribute towards stability. Those who undermine stability in the pursuit of dubious democratic rights; those who ignore the well-being of the majority cannot be considered as having the interest of their country or even of democracy at heart. It is for these reasons that communists and extremists are not allowed to use democratic processes in order to destroy democracy.

AIPO has a role to play in promoting better understanding of the limitations and responsibilities of democracy as much as it must promote the benefits to be derived from the system.

I hope that this assembly will contribute towards the betterment of Asean countries in particular and developing countries in general.

12

Need for Asean to Work Closely in Agriculture

"Agriculture is still the mainstay of the majority of the economies of Asean member countries. It still provides employment and livelihood to a majority of our populace, and as a common feature, the agricultural sector as a whole is still faced with problems of poverty and malnutrition."

ASEAN has emerged as a strong regional grouping committed to maintaining political and economic stability in the region through cooperative endeavours among its member nations. Apart from resolving issues of political consequences to the stability of the region, economic cooperation in the

---

A speech delivered at the 10th Meeting of the Asean Ministers of Agriculture and Forestry in Kuala Lumpur, Malaysia, on October 20, 1988

field of agriculture, fisheries and forestry assume special significance within Asean. Agriculture is still the mainstay of the majority of the economies of Asean member countries. It still provides employment and livelihood to a majority of our populace, and as a common feature, the agricultural sector as a whole is still faced with problems of poverty and malnutrition.

In Malaysia for example, though it is putting greater emphasis on the manufacturing industries, rural and consequently agricultural development is still a subject of high priority. The objective in rural development has been and continues to be the redressal of poverty among the rural population made up of subsistence farmers, smallholders, fishermen and landless agricultural workers.

Urban poverty does exist and it would be grossly unfair and unjust not to recognise it and to ameliorate it. But poverty in the developing countries is largely rural and involves agriculturists. The belief that mere redistribution of land would overcome rural poverty has not been fully proven. Even where land is owned by the tillers of the soil extreme poverty persists. If the developing countries are going to rely on agriculture, and they must if they want to avoid hunger, then they must reexamine their agricultural practices in order that they do not impoverish the farmers who supply them with food.

Asean, like many other developing countries, have not neglected agriculture or rural development. We can be justly proud of the notable achievements that have been made in technical as well as economic cooperation in our region. However, much more can be done if we could strengthen our cooperation in the area of agricultural practices and trade. We have a need to learn from each other and to present a more united front when dealing with the developed world, our major market. It is not a cartel that we should propose but it is important to remember that the developed countries are getting closer together and they will soon adopt a single policy or approach in their trade with us.

The contribution of the industrialised countries towards the development of third world countries is well recognised. The developed or industrialised countries have done much in providing technical assistance to the developing countries in order to accelerate rural development. But developing countries need money with which to develop. Although aid, both technical and financial, can help, in the final analysis it is equitable trade which will enable rural poverty to be reduced. As the rural areas are agricultural, trade in agricultural produce means a great deal not only to a developing country but to the farmers themselves.

Presently, the economic activities of the developing countries are adversely affected by the economic policies and trade practices of the industrialised countries. Among these are manipulation of food surpluses in the rich industrial countries, control over commodity trading and prices and protectionist policies which have direct and adverse consequences on the economies of the developing countries.

In recent years, food surpluses in the rich industrialised countries have increased tremendously because massive farm subsidies tend to encourage farmers to produce more and more. That their local market cannot absorb what they produce seems of little concern to them. They are even less concerned with the disruption they cause in the international market where their surplus is sold at below cost. Unable to compete in this environment, the farmers of developing countries are doomed to poverty. Technically they are less efficient but it is the distortions caused by massive subsidies in developed countries which is killing them, frequently literally.

If indeed the developing countries are to progress in the true sense of the word, then the apparent contradiction, of on the one hand helping developing countries to increase their outputs while, on the other hand, denying them market outlets, must be overcome. Asean as a grouping of developing countries still dependent on agriculture must work closely together in the GATT rounds of talks in order to persuade the developed North to adhere to the understanding on standstill and rollback of subsidies for farmers. It is worthwhile to note that developing countries like Malaysia not only deny subsidies for agricultural production but impose cess and export duties on them.

To my mind, Asean, as a regional grouping, must address this problem in a determined and concerted manner. In this connection, future collaborative efforts in the field of agriculture and forestry should not stop purely at agro-technical fields, but must also be geared towards obtaining more favarouble trade arrangements for the benefit of member countries.

Asean's agricultural trade has traditionally been based on the export of primary commodities. In the past few years, we have seen how the decline in prices of commodities in the world market have depressed agricultural commodity trading and affected our respective economies. The declining commodity prices have affected the terms of trade so much that for the same amount of manufactured goods from the developed countries we have to sell two to three times more of the commodities we export. Additionally we are meeting more and more unethical trade practices on the part of powerful competitors from the North. The cost of countering such unfair practices is so high that alone we will fall one by one. The need to cooperate is therefore more urgent now.

Regional interests aside, Asean must lend support to global efforts at eliminating protectionism. To this end, Asean must support the MTN-Uruguay Rounds which is to be held for a period of four years beginning this year. There is no denying that the Uruguay Rounds is of special interest to us as it involves negotiations with other member countries of the General Agreement on Trade and Tariffs (GATT) for the purpose of eliminating protectionism. As you are all aware, the Uruguay Rounds was specially called for by the Ministerial Declaration at the Special Meeting on MTN in Punta Del Este in September 1986 in view of the increasing number of GATT member countries that are exercising protectionist policies.

It is relevant to mention here that the group on agriculture has carried out several rounds of negotiations in Geneva, but without much encouraging results so far. This has been largely due to the posture adopted by certain highly industrialised countries with regard to the approach in reducing subsidies in the production and trading of agricultural commodities.

Nonetheless, I am happy to note that the "Cairns Group", of which Malaysia is a member, is currently working on a proposal which the group feels will be acceptable to the developed countries concerned. The proposal will be submitted for Ministerial approval at the Mid-Term Review of the Uruguay Rounds scheduled to be held in Montreal, Canada in December this year. Hopefully, this effort will lead to the liberalisation of agricultural trade at the international level in the long run.

13

The Impact of a Changing World on Asean-European Community Relations

"The momentous changes that are taking place are going to affect Asean-E.C. relations. If we value our relations, if we see it as making an important contribution to global stability and prosperity then we must seek to ensure that the changes confronting us work to strengthen our relations."

WE meet here at a momentous time in the history of the world. In the Asia-Pacific region we are witnessing the dawn of the Pacific Age with high growth rates, expanding economies and greater regional economic cooperation. Japan has

---

A speech delivered at the 8th Asean-European Community Ministerial Meeting in Kuching, Sarawak, Malaysia, on February 16, 1990

become an economic superpower in its own right and is set to chart a global political course of its own.

The U.S., long the main engine of world growth, is facing serious economic challenges. Its free trade agreement with Canada, however, has created a major new trading bloc with all the implications that trading blocs have.

In Europe, the European Community (E.C.) is gearing up to realise Project 1992, the single European market. Close cooperation between the E.C. and the European Free Trade Association (EFTA) is also in the offing. In the Soviet Union *perestroika* and *glasnost* continue to initiate changes that would have been unimaginable only months ago. Even more unthinkable are the radical changes occurring in Eastern Europe as a result of the Soviet decision not to prop up the governments.

Since we meet within the context of an Asean-E.C. forum I would like to confine my remarks principally to the impact of these changes on our mutual relationship. The momentous changes that are taking place are going to affect Asean-E.C. relations. If we value our relations, if we see it as making an important contribution to global stability and prosperity then we must seek to ensure that the changes confronting us work to strengthen our relations.

Undoubtedly the E.C. will enter the 1990s with an enhanced economic and political role. It is going to emerge from Project 1992 as the most powerful economic and political grouping.

A reinvigorated and resurgent Europe has implications for Asean and the rest of the world. Will the establishment of an internal market and other integrative measures mean a more inward-looking E.C., content on trading within itself and the European

Economic Space which would include the EFTA countries? In 1987, for example, 60 per cent of total E.C. exports went to the E.C. countries and if EFTA is included, E.C. exports to European destinations was as high as 70 per cent. The potential is there for an inward looking and less open trading group. If we add Eastern Europe as well, the E.C. might well do without the rest of the world.

While the E.C. may consider the Asean area as an important investment centre and the establishment of the E.C. joint-investment committees in each Asean capital attests to that, the attitude of the investors is somewhat different. Despite the very attractive packages and incentives offered by Asean countries, European investors still have a preference for the industrialised nations in the E.C., and North America. After 1992 they might even be more disinclined to venture outwards to Asean and seek instead the advantages of a homogeneous and enlarged market. This is an aspect which I hope you will take up at this meeting bearing in mind the high priority accorded to closer industrial cooperation at the 7th Asean-E.C. Ministerial Meeting in Dusseldorf in May 1989.

Asean's concern about developments in the internal market are real because not only is the E.C. a significant source for development funding, it is also the third largest trading partner of Asean after Japan and the U.S. In 1987 the E.C. accounted for 13 per cent of Asean's global exports and 14 per cent of Asean's global imports.

How would this trade be affected come 1992? There may be a free flow of goods, people, services and capital within the community and a conducive atmosphere for healthy growth and competition. But for those outside the E.C. they will have to adjust to a whole new set of policies and regulations on banking, trading and public procurement. While efforts are being made by the E.C. to provide more transparency to what is taking place, it will be some time before our business and trading community will fully comprehend and familiarise itself with the new business environment.

Furthermore all decisions on the regulatory aspects of trade are being taken without any discussion with the E.C.'s trading partners. Hence it is natural that there be apprehension as to whether we would still be facing national quotas and under what conditions and whether our products will continue to have market access to the E.C. We hear that GSP provisions will be done away with in favour of common tariffs for all imports.

There is obviously an 'information gap' here which both Asean and the E.C. have tried to fill by organising colloquiums, seminars and meetings. However, project 1992 is an immense and complex enterprise. More contacts between the two sides are necessary particularly in assisting our exporters who would be most affected by the changes.

There also appears to be a 'consistency gap' between the E.C.'s position as a leading proponent of trade liberalisation and multilateralism, on the one hand, and what it does to further the cause of these principles on the other. It is necessary for the E.C. to demonstrate that the principles of free trade and competition do not stop short at its borders but will be applicable to all in a fair, just and equitable manner.

Nowhere is the application of these principles more relevant than in the current Uruguay Round of the Multilateral Trade Negotiations which seem to be stalled in the various groups on tariffs, tropical products and agriculture. Many of the issues which are being dealt with in these groups are of vital importance to Asean and other developing countries. We would like the E.C. to show the political will necessary to get the negotiations moving towards a successful outcome.

I hope this meeting here in Kuching will help reassure us that far from being 'Fortress Europe' the E.C. will not only maintain but strengthen its relations with Asean and will play an active role in support of the open multilateral trading system.

In rapid succession the regimes of Eastern Europe have collapsed under the pressure of mass demonstrations and mass dissatisfaction. The people of Eastern Europe are now enthusiastically pursuing their goals of a more democratic and prosperous society.

As a democratic and free-enterprise nation Malaysia welcomes the recent changes in Eastern Europe. We welcome the changes because it will also enhance both European and global security and stability. In addition it will provide new opportunities for trade and economic cooperation for all.

Eastern Europe, however, still faces many challenges ahead. Eastern Europe is going to need a lot of help and support. Malaysia and Asean will not grudge Eastern Europe this support. Indeed, we too would like to assist Eastern Europe in whatever way we can.

Developments in the Soviet Union and in Eastern Europe have already had a positive effect on the Asia-Pacific region. Both Soviet and U.S. forces are being reduced. This improvement in the overall politico-strategic situation will in turn offer Asean new regional opportunities to pursue our long-cherished goal of a Zone of Peace, Freedom and Neutrality (ZOPFAN) and allow for an even greater focus on economic development.

But like you, we also have our fears and concerns. Fears have been expressed that large-scale Western assistance to Eastern Europe will be at the expense of other developing countries. In raising this issue here I want to emphasise that I am not making a plea for assistance to Asean *per se*. I plead rather for the many Third World countries who are facing serious economic and social difficulties. I think we all accept the fact that economic development is a vital factor in promoting peace and stability.

The question in our mind is whether Eastern Europe will now draw away the already sparse inflow of European investments into Southeast Asia. Despite assurances that more would be done to encourage greater investments in Asean, European investments continue to lag behind those from other regions.

In the area of trade the situation is equally less reassuring. It would be disastrous for us if a combination of the 1992 Single Market and special trading privileges for Eastern Europe lead to diminished market access for Asean exports.

Western Europe has therefore a unique and historic opportunity not just to mould the future of Eastern Europe but also the future of the world as well. You can create opportunities for Asean countries, and others, to join with you in the reconstruction and development of Eastern Europe and indeed of other regions as well. You can also help to bring together businessmen and business opportunities in a three way link-up between Western Europe, Eastern Europe and Asean. You can also help by ensuring that your single market, will lead to greater international cooperation and to an upsurge of international trade that will benefit all nations. Peace and progress in Europe cannot be pursued separately from peace and progress elsewhere in the world.

Let me now take up some issues nearer home. We in Malaysia view with great concern the campaign currently being waged against us on the issue of tropical rainforests. We have seen how these campaigns have resulted in the boycott of tropical timber in some E.C. countries.

We recognise that there are many organisations, groups and individuals who are genuinely concerned about the environment. However, there are those who are bent on carrying out their campaigns based on sentiments and irrationality. And when they have the ears of political parties either in power or in the opposition, biased policies emerge. Action is often taken against us not because it is deemed right but because it is popular. While this may be a vote-catching issue for some, for us in the developing countries, it is a matter of economic survival.

The timber industry plays an important role in the Malaysian economy. In 1988 it constituted 5.1 per cent of Malaysia's total export earnings and gave direct employment to 162,000 people. There is every indication that the timber industry is poised to make a bigger contribution to the economy as we concentrate on value-added products, particularly furniture-making. Industrialised countries could assist us in these efforts by lowering their protective walls currently in place against such manufactured products. At the moment, the tariff barriers in some countries favour sawn timber and logs against finished higher value products. The irony is that this not only retards our industrialisation process but it also encourages more trees to be felled. If the environmentalists are truly concerned they should encourage relocation of timber-based industries into the timber producing countries. That way employment and foreign exchange earnings will be sustained with less timber felling. A boycott of tropical timber may result in the clearing of more forest land for agriculture and development.

The Asean countries collectively have over 170 million hectares of tropical forests. This represents more than half of the total land area of Asean. In Malaysia, our tropical rainforests cover about 20 million hectares, out of a total land area of 33 million hectares, or about 61 per cent. If you take into account tree crops such as rubber, oil palm and cocoa, the area under forest and tree crops comes up to nearly 74 per cent of the total area. Considering that nearly a hundred years have passed since we first started clearing our jungles to make way for plantation agriculture, you will appreciate that far from indiscriminately clearing our forests as alleged, much care and planning have gone into managing our forests. Long before it became fashionable for those in the West to espouse the cause of the rainforests, we in Malaysia were already actively engaged in managing our forest resources and in preserving our wildlife and biological diversity.

What we would now like to see is the discussion being carried to a more constructive level so that the focus is on joint efforts by both the developed and the developing countries to protect the environment while pursuing the twin objectives of economic growth and sustainable development. The Langkawi Declaration adopted by the Commonwealth Heads of Government Meeting in Kuala Lumpur recently, could form a useful basis for such action by both Asean and the E.C.

And now let me touch briefly on the so-called issue of the Penans about which two resolutions have already been adopted by the European Parliament. You could not have met at a more appropriate place to know more about this matter.

For now, let me emphasise one point clearly: we do not intend to turn the Penans into "human zoological specimens" to be gawked at by tourists and studied by anthropologists while the rest of the world passes them by. The Penans in question number about 900 out of a total Penan population of about 9,000 in Sarawak. While the majority of them have successfully settled, the remainder are still leading nomadic lives in the jungle. It is our policy to eventually bring all jungle dwellers into the mainstream of the nation's life. There is nothing romantic about these helpless, half-starved and disease-ridden people and we will make no apologies for endeavouring to uplift their living conditions. I hope during your stay in Sarawak you will be able to appreciate the situation better.

You also have the question of drugs on your agenda and rightly so. Asean-E.C. cooperation is an essential part of the international effort to combat drug abuse and illicit trafficking. Malaysia, on its part, has adopted a mixture of harsh measures against traffickers and mandatory rehabilitation for drug users to meet this challenge head on. As a result the spread of drug abuse here is much less than in the more tolerant countries, where the spread of drug abuse is much more and with greater speed. There must be no let up in our war on drug abuse.

It is heartening to note that countries have pledged their political support for more intensified cooperation on all fronts. The 1987 International Conference on Drug Abuse and Illicit Trafficking in Vienna laid that foundation. Hopefully, the U.N. General Assembly's Special Session on Drugs which is to be held in a few days time will carry the fight forward for a concerted programme of action involving both the producer and consumer countries. Asean-E.C. cooperation on this issue must also move forward. Drug traffickers must know that we are determined to leave them no place to thrive or to enjoy their ill-gotten gains.

Recent initiatives on the Cambodian issue have given us fresh hope for progress in finding a peaceful political settlement. The central point in these initiatives is an enhanced United Nations role in Cambodia. The decision of the five permanent members of the U.N. Security Council to be collectively and directly seized of the matter is certainly significant. The Australian proposal can also form the basis in our search for a political settlement. I welcome the convening of the Informal Meeting on Cambodia in Jakarta at the end of this month. Malaysia will contribute positively to this peace process.

While our attention is focussed on the developments concerning Cambodia we must not marginalise the problem of the Vietnamese boat people. For 14 years Malaysia and other Southeast Asian countries have for humanitarian considerations accorded temporary refuge to the Vietnamese boat people. Increasingly, this asylum facility is being abused by Vietnamese seeking a better life in Western countries. Their continuing influx has exerted unacceptable pressures on our social and political fabric. Malaysia believes that a durable solution to this problem is obtainable in the Comprehensive Plan of Action (CPA) provided all its aspects are implemented in totality and simultaneously. We cannot accept being singled out to shoulder the burden. In the first instance we were not, even indirectly, the cause of the problem. It is therefore incumbent on the international community and particularly those adopting high moral positions to ensure the full and immediate implementation of the CPA.

14

Asean and the World Economy: The Challenge of Change

"... the course that the states of Asean must take cannot just be to let others shape that history. We cannot be mere objects of international relations. With the 'East' in turmoil, the 'South' in continuing crisis, and the 'West' on an economic collision course, an active Asean can contribute positively."

DESPITE the Age of Confrontation and Cold War being behind us we still do not seem to know where we are going. Our future history is very much in the making with no clear indication as to the direction it will take.

A speech delivered at the International Conference on Asean Countries and the World Economy in Bali, Indonesia, on March 4, 1991

At this crucial turning point, the course that the states of Asean must take cannot just be to let others shape that history. We cannot be mere objects of international relations. With the 'East' in turmoil, the 'South' in continuing crisis, and the 'West' on an economic collision course, an active Asean can contribute positively. It is incumbent upon us to play a productive role in the making of the new international economic order.

This is a time, therefore, for the most creative Asean initiatives for a productive peace. Our joint collaboration must go beyond our Asean subregion, beyond the region of Southeast Asia, beyond East Asia, even beyond the Pacific region.

We must of course be aware of our limited weight in the international arena. There is every reason for humility. But the corruption arising from a sense of powerlessness is as bad as the corruption of power.

If we do not in our own modest ways try to shape history, then we must not bemoan our fate later.

In the last two generations, too much of the creative energies and resources of the world were diverted from possible cooperation to deadly East-West confrontation, from the task of enhancing the prosperity of the world's peoples to the pursuit of national security imperatives. Too much of the world's resources were diverted to conflict, diverted away from the demands of development.

We have seen the spread of democracy and democratic tendencies, most spectacularly, of course, in Eastern Europe. Democracy may mean freedom from political oppression but not necessarily from economic and developmental oppression. The proponents of democracy are not averse to international dictatorship.

The process of turning battlefields into marketplaces is continuing apace.

Throughout the world, most dramatically of course in what was once called the Socialist Bloc, we see a swing towards the free-enterprise system. The collapse of communism as an ideology and the command economy as an economic method and the turn towards the market system, can contribute towards higher productivity nationally and greater prosperity for the entire global economic system.

But at the same time, we would be extremely foolish not to be fully aware of the negative side of the equation.

There is today an economic recession in the U.S., Canada, Australia, New Zealand and the United Kingdom democracy and the free market notwithstanding. Japan and Germany have slowed down. In the 1960s, the OECD countries, on which so much of Asean's economic performance is hinged, grew by an annual average of 5 per cent. In the 1970s, they grew on average by 3.1 per cent a year; in the 1980s by an average of 2.9 per cent. Whereas there is every hope that the recession economies will not be down for long, we would be foolish to predicate our future on a vigorous and fast growing world economy.

In the 1990s we must also expect international trade to grow at a less than robust rate. This again will be no surprise given that in the 1960s world trade grew annually by an average of 8 per cent, in the 1970s by 6 per cent, in the 1980s by 4.4 per cent.

A less than vigorous trade growth regime in the foreseeable future should also be no great surprise given the rise of protectionism and managed trade, the movement towards trade blocs, and the general erosion of the global trading system. We can only hope that GATT will not in the end stand for a general agreement to talk and talk and no more than that.

Real commodity prices will continue their downward trend and will offer no relief to heavily-indebted developing countries that are still dependent on the exports of agricultural and other raw materials. The global debt crisis too will not go away.

There is a danger of a global credit squeeze arising out of the diversion of German financial flows to the eastern part of Germany and Eastern Europe, the reduced surpluses of Japan, the sustained high deficits of the U.S., the problems of the banking and financial system in Japan, the U.S. and elsewhere, and the investment of Japanese surpluses increasingly in their own domestic development.

There are a host of problems for the world arising out of the structural weaknesses of the world's biggest economy and biggest debtor nation, the U.S. We now live in a world where the developing countries are deprived of the past leverage of "defection to the other side". There is the sole American giant, with immense problems at home and no longer driven by the imperatives of the Cold War abroad. We must surely expect a more demanding U.S., desirous of greater "help" and "adjustment" from others.

We see a situation today of a dramatic rise in the political, diplomatic and military clout of the U.S. and a severe erosion in its economic position and welfare. We can expect the application of that enhanced political, diplomatic and military clout to shore up the economic position and to enhance the U.S.'s economic welfare. The increased pressures will be political and social as well as economic. Military adventures cannot be excluded.

We cannot rightly expect the clash of the economic giants—the U.S., Japan and the European Community—to attenuate. We should expect it to escalate, making it incumbent upon us to make sure that we are not squeezed in the middle, and caught in the cross-fire.

We should take into our calculations the possibility of greater Eurocentricism, and a greater E.C. to include the Eastern European countries. We must expect continuing and serious instability in the previously tightly controlled states of the Soviet Socialist Republics and Eastern Europe.

This rough balance sheet of longer-term positive and negative fundamentals and uncertainties reminds me of the very first paragraph of Charles Dickens's *A Tale of Two Cities*, a tale of courage and adventure set against the tumultuous era of the French Revolution. Let me quote the entire paragraph, written in one long sentence, to describe Europe in 1775. Dickens wrote of that period:

> "It was the best of times, it was the worst of times, it was the age of wisdom, it was the age of foolishness, it was the epoch of belief, it was the epoch of incredulity, it was the season of Light, it was the season of Darkness, it was the spring of hope, it was the winter of despair, we had everything before us, we had nothing before us, we were all going direct to Heaven, we were all going direct the other way—in short, the period was so far like the present period, that some of its noisiest authorities insisted on its being received, for good or for evil, in the superlative degree of comparison only."

I believe that what Dickens wrote of the Europe of 1775 is superlatively apt in describing our world of the early 1990s. It is indeed the best of times and the worst of times. It is indeed the age of wisdom and the age of foolishness. It is indeed the epoch of belief and the epoch of incredulity. It is indeed the season of Light and the season of Darkness. It is indeed the spring of hope and the winter of despair. We do indeed have everything before us and nothing before us.

In the case of Europe after 1775, there was an era of turmoil and devastation, culminating in the Napoleonic Wars. Order was only restored with the Congress of Vienna of 1814-1815.

Our world today cannot afford two generations of turmoil. And Asean must contribute to the collaborative peace, through balanced economic development worldwide.

Globally there is a chance for a more effective and productive United Nations. Asean should act in concert to ensure that the United Nations develops into an even-handed global authority, the conscience of all mankind and protector of the weak against the aggression of the strong. We should work together to make sure that the United Nations is reinvigorated and will serve to deny Thucydide's Conclusion: "that in the affairs of states, the strong will demand what they will and the weak must yield what they must."

The Asean countries and many developing nations which are so dependent on an open trading system—much more dependent than any of the great trading nations such as Japan, Germany and the U.S.—must make the GATT system work. The tide of protectionism must be halted and rolled back. The movement towards mercantilist, inward-looking, and "the rest of the world be damned" trading blocs must be reversed. The trend towards managed trade, bilateralism and unilateralism, must be stopped dead in its tracks. Asean must help to secure the open trading system that will save not just ourselves but the very nations which are busy erecting trade barriers.

However, before Asean can hope to influence the economic course of the world, we must strengthen Asean itself, all the three parts of Asean. We must strengthen the Asean Peace, the Asean Concert and the web of economic and social relationship between us in the Asean Community.

First, the Pax Aseana which we have successfully constructed since the mid-1960s must not be taken for granted. It has been one of the great successes of the postwar world, the more remarkable because it has been a Pax without an Imperium. The statesmenship of the founding fathers will be prominently recorded in the history of the region. The leadership of Asean will be required in the days ahead to strengthen the Asean Peace. We would be very foolish to take for granted the structure of understanding, mutual respect, trust and goodwill that has been established. The Asean Peace must be an active peace, which must be in constant upkeep, and in perpetual construction.

Second, the Asean Concert, our joining of hands to deal with the outside world. The wide agenda for Asean initiative cannot be actualised without a substantial strengthening of the Asean Concert in the days ahead, when the "Cambodia cement" and the defensive anti-communist impulse will recede further into history.

Third, we must indeed launch bold and innovative initiatives with regard to enhancing the level of economic cooperation between us. We should aspire to achieve a level of performance on the economic front that we have secured with regard to our political and diplomatic cooperation.

There is now a clear Asean consensus on the strengthening of the Asean Secretariat, to enable it to respond to the challenge of internal cooperation and the challenges of external action in the 1990s. We must quickly turn consensus into concrete reality.

Much will have to be done at the 4th Asean Summit that will be held in Singapore. And much will need to be accomplished in the run-up to the Summit. With regard to this, I believe it is time for Asean to consider a new element, an Asean Informal Meeting of Heads of State which should meet regularly in a relaxed ambience between the formal Summit Meetings. Such an informal gathering, away from the cameras and the pressure to produce some dramatic out-come, held for the purpose of merely exchanging views and perspectives and keeping in close touch, would contribute to the process of ensuring fullest consultation between us. This should be over and above the bilateral meetings. I believe that it cannot be stressed enough that we of Asean at all levels must be engaged in a constant process of candid consultation.

Let me now turn to a broader geographical canvas: what Asean should now be actively considering with regard to Southeast Asia. International relations in Southeast Asia has moved from a situation of warm war to cold war. We have now progressed to a cold peace. It is time to move our relationship towards a cooperative peace.

The time has come for Asean to prepare for the making of a new Southeast Asia. Asean must move forward with the creative and comprehensive engagement of the other states of the region.

Southeast Asia should no longer be at sixes and threes. The mountain of distrust and misunderstanding must be removed. A divided region is not in the interest of any regional state. It is in the interest of all of Southeast Asia that we secure a system composed of states which are economically prosperous, socially dynamic, strategically secure, domestically at peace and politically unpolarised. The Asean states should act now to hammer out the acceptable modalities and the most appropriate mechanisms.

In 1967, we together launched the first act of regional reconciliation. The outcome was Asean.

We must now stand ready to launch the second phase of regional reconciliation, to achieve the objective Asean set out from the moment of its birth: the creation of a Southeast Asian system of states that are at peace with each other, involved in a dynamic and vigorous economic and political relationship of mutual respect and mutually beneficial cooperation.

Asean now already has Bali's Treaty of Amity and Cooperation in Southeast Asia which sets out the fundamental precepts for political, economic, social, technical and scientific cooperation between us. Papua New Guinea, among the non-members of Asean, has acceded to the Treaty. Asean should now welcome any initiative taken by any of the regional states to accede to this admirable and comprehensive treaty.

The idea of inviting initially the foreign ministers of Vietnam, Laos and Myanmar to a dialogue with the Asean Foreign Ministers, and the Heads of Government of these countries to a dialogue at the next Asean Summit has also been put forward. These are suggestions that should be given serious study. In the meantime, let me inform you that the Malaysian government encourages the fullest private sector participation in the economies of the non-Asean states of Southeast Asia. Southeast Asia is now no longer a battleground. Let us proceed as fast as we possibly can to turn it into one prosperous marketplace.

Let me now turn to the proposal for an East Asian Economic Grouping (EAEG).

In the first place let me emphasise that the Group is not intended to be a trade bloc. Regional economic groupings are acknowledged as legitimate means for neighbours in a region to improve their economic well-being. Accordingly preferential treatment and the removal of trade barriers within a group are legitimate and proper.

But a grouping becomes a trade bloc when the member states are no longer allowed to negotiate trading terms on their own with nations outside the group. The European Community claims that it is not a trade bloc but the fact is that even now import quotas and preferential treatment are based not on the requirement of individual member countries but on the E.C. as a whole. In 1992 this will be formalised and there is justifiable fear that trade between the E.C. countries will be classified as domestic with all that that implies and quotas will be fixed for imports from outside of Europe, quotas designed to protect the industries and agricultural produce of Europe as a whole.

The U.S. for its part has entered into a free trade union with Canada and will shortly do the same with Mexico. The U.S.'s declared objective is to make the whole of North, Central and South America a single economic grouping. The degree of exclusivity in trade that will result from this grouping is as yet a matter of speculation but such a grouping cannot but be protectionist to a degree.

The countries of Europe and America have a reputation for economic arm twisting, though not always by governments. Thus "human rights" records, trade unionism, exchange rates, media treatment, environment protection, "democratic practices", quality and health standards and a host of other issues are used for the suppression of the economic growth of potential competitors. The action taken against the so-called NICs are illustrative of this. Alone and bereft of friendly support, these countries are not in a position to even protest. Indeed, open protest might invite even more severe punitive pressures.

It is paradoxical that even as the centrally planned Eastern bloc economies espouse the free-market systems as a solution to their economic problem, the erstwhile free traders of the west are opting for a controlled international marketing system. But the fact is that with the formation of the European Union (E.U.) and the American free trading zone, that is what is happening.

The question is what do we in this region do to rescue the free trading system of the world? Do we refuse to acknowledge the gloomy facts? Do we hush up things? Do we look the other way? Do we accept them without a whimper? Or do we confront them; the reality of those trade blocs, that is, not the nations.

Two wrongs do not make one right. We in East Asia must not form a trading bloc of our own. But we know that alone and singly we cannot stop the slide towards controlled and regulated international commerce; which in fact is no different from the command economies of the socialist soviets, only the scale is international; which is obviously going to replace free trade if the E.C. and the American Union are allowed to rewrite the rules. To stop the slide and to preserve free trade the countries of East Asia, which contain some of the most dynamic economies in the world today, must at least speak with one voice.

It will be impossible to do this unless we can consult each other, unless we can have some form of grouping which is recognisable. A free trade arrangement between us is impossible at this point in time. There is too much disparity in our development. An Economic Community after the E.C. pattern is far too structured and is well nigh impossible to achieve. But a formal grouping intended to facilitate consultation and consensus prior to negotiating with Europe or America or in multilateral fora such as the GATT is not too far-fetched an idea. It is also not against the GATT principle, nor will it run contrary to membership in such organisations as the Asia-Pacific Economic Cooperation (APEC), in which the U.S. and Canada are members while having an economic union with each other.

Because of its market size alone, the EAEG will be listened to. But it will also have the knowledge, the technology and the skills which can become bargaining counters in any trade off with the trading blocs of Europe and America.

Membership of the Group by developing countries should serve to remind the other members of their responsibility to the developing world. A concerted effort can then be made to boost the economic growth of the weaker members, and indeed to help the developing world generally.

The mere existence of the group, backed as it is by the massive combined economic strength of the members should help to retard the slide towards trade blocs and protectionism. At the same time the group can foster better trade and development within the group. Given a dedication towards mutual help, the Group can survive without the constrictive structuring of a formal economic community.

After the initial negativism following the mooting of the Group, it is heartening that lately there have been more positive pronouncements from Europe and America. The members of Asean now understand the EAEG concept and support it. What remains is for us to formally propose the concept to the East Asian nations outside of Asean. This is a task for all Asean nations.

I am sure that once it is understood that the EAEG is principally concerned with trade and the maintenance of free trade, that it does not compete with the Asean group, that it is GATT and even APEC compatible, the fears regarding its formation and its role will disappear. World trade would benefit from EAEG rather than be stifled by it.

As I said at the beginning, the peace dividend that should come with the ending of the East-West confrontation is not with us yet. Indeed, the situation is very fluid, with signs of recession everywhere and new centres of tension and instability.

In espousing democracy and free enterprise, nations are finding that it is easier to declare the intention, or to overthrow authoritarian regimes even, than to obtain tangible benefits from democratic freedom and the market economy.

Peoples power is fine. It can remove dictators and corrupt governments. But power corrupts and peoples power can be no less corrupting. Once it is realised that political power can be achieved through getting people on to the streets, the potentially corrupt can also resort to this weapon for their own ends. Indeed, the overthrow of the corrupt often results in the installation of another leader who is or becomes equally corrupt. It is easier to overthrow allegedly corrupt government than to materialise a government that can rehabilitate the nation.

Democracy must not be an end in itself. It must remain a means to an end—the installation of good governments in the true sense of the word. Making a religion of democracy, accepting everything that is done in its name unquestioningly will only destroy the faith in the efficacy of the system. Forcing it down the throat of people who are not ready for it will not do any good either.

To succeed, democracy has to become a culture of the people. Its shortcomings must be recognised and accepted and circumspection must be applied to it as with every system of government.

The end of the Cold War and East-West confrontation and the universal acceptance of the liberal democracy concept are to be welcomed but the dividend can only come if we appreciate the need to organise and arrange the system that will replace confrontation. There will be no dividend if in the affairs of nations the Thucydide's Conclusion still apply: "that the strong will demand what they will and the weak must yield what they must."

15

Asean: Good Return of Growth and Stability

"The Asean experiences have shown that when countries in a region consult and cooperate, their chances of stability and success are greater. It is no accident that the Asean countries have such good records of economic growth and political stability."

WE meet here at a momentous time in the history of the world in which events at the losing years of this century will rewrite the equation of political and economic balance in the emerging new world order. No other period during this century holds such promise of reconciliation and cooperation, for with

---

A speech delivered at the 24th Asean Ministerial Meeting in Kuala Lumpur, Malaysia, on July 19, 1991

the end of the Cold War the age of East-West division has ended. Unfortunately, new uncertainties have arisen which threaten to erode the open global trading system.

While we applaud the reduction in East-West tensions and the dramatic speed at which the socialist countries have opted for democracy and the free enterprise system, we view with disquiet and growing concern the trade disputes between the economic super-powers—the U.S., Japan and the European Community. Another political and economic reality of the world today is the trend towards closed regionalism. Managed trade, bilateralism and trading based on reciprocity endanger the open multilateral trading system, and consequently the growth of world trade.

The stalemate of the Uruguay Round, the growing competition for market access and new adverse trade practices are ominous signs that discriminative economics and exclusionary trading policies will characterise the relations between the groupings of the developed world as well as between the developed and the developing world.

The economies of Asean and the many developing nations which are so dependent upon the open trading system are threatened by the new waves of protectionism. It is to defend the open multilateral trading system that the formation of an East Asian Economic Grouping (EAEG) has been proposed. The EAEG mirrors our basic belief in close consultation and cooperation between regional countries for the common good. It also reflects Asean's concern over the spread of regional trading blocs and constitutes a realistic approach to counter the adversarial and protectionistic stance adopted by some countries and economic groups which is putting the multilateral trading system in jeopardy.

Let me stress that the EAEG is not a trade bloc but the concept is that of a loose consultative forum comprising countries in East Asia. The EAEG will provide Asean and other East Asian countries the leverage and a platform to act in concert and speak with one voice with regard to any trade problems or trade-related issues that affect us directly or indirectly. It will not work to restrict or constrict trade. On the contrary, its imperatives will be the defence and maintenance of free trade and expansion of economic relations between regional countries as well as with those outside the region.

The Asean experiences have shown that when countries in a region consult and cooperate, their chances of stability and success are greater. It is no accident that the Asean countries have such good records of economic growth and political stability. Clearly an extension of such consultation and cooperation to encompass the countries of East Asia will have the same effect. Not only will the Zone of Peace, Freedom and Neutrality (ZOPFAN) be served but by helping the weaker economies of East Asia to grow, intraregional trade will grow and the problems of economic migration resolved.

Asean and the other East Asian countries, whether economically strong or weak, need an anchor to weather and withstand the adverse trade winds which are blowing. A strong and united Asean, politically as well as economically, can bring the EAEG into shape and make it work for the positive benefit of all. The EAEG would be Asean's contribution to the maintenance of an open global trading system.

The West tells us that democratic freedom and human rights are fundamental for the achievement of economic and social development. We in Asean never disputed that democracy for the people and opportunity for the individual to develop his or her own greatest potentials are indeed important principles. We disagree, however, that democracy has only one definition or that political systems qualify as democratic only when they measure up to certain particular yardsticks. Similarly, the norms and precepts for the observance of human rights vary from society to society and from one period to another within the same society.

Therefore, when the issue of human rights are linked to trade, investment and finance we cannot but view them as added conditionalities and protectionism by other means. We question whether the motivations have not in fact been political and self-serving. Malaysia now faces a petition by the International Labor Rights, Education and Research Fund (ILRERF) to withdraw our trade privileges under the U.S.'s GSP. They say Malaysia has violated workers' rights and freedoms. This is not the first of such petitions and will not be the last. The American Federation of Labor-Congress of Industrial Organisation (AFL-CIO) mounted similar petitions before. These labour organisations may seem to be concerned with the welfare of our workers but should their petitions result in the withdrawal of GSP privileges, the net result will be to reduce investments in our country and create unemployment among the workers. We should recognise their actions for what they really are.

Governments in developing countries constantly face the problem of securing a fine balance between the need to ensure national economic development and the kind of individual and group disruptive activities which tend to destabilise society and inhibit growth. Nobody can claim to have the monopoly of wisdom to determine what is right and proper for all countries and peoples. It would be condescending, to say the least, and suspect for the West to preach human rights to us in the East.

In the Asean experience, we have learnt that both at the national and regional levels, peace and security, democracy and freedom as well as stability are possible and sustainable only when the people are free from economic deprivation and have a stake in the national life. Rightly, Asean countries have placed a high premium on political stability by managing a balance between the rights of the individual and the needs of the society as a whole. This has enabled the Asean countries to make great strides in the socioeconomic advancement of their peoples. It has also enhanced the resilience of individual countries and the Asean region as a whole. However, Asean needs to do more.

Asean is 24 years old this year. It is cohesive, united by shared geography, common goals and economic dynamism. It is today much envied by many. Its success in providing a climate of peace and stability has enabled its member states to concentrate on economic development, resulting in our economies being among the fastest growing in the Asia-Pacific region. We achieved a growth rate of about 8 per cent in 1990, a record that we are all proud of and must strive to maintain, if not to improve.

However, we cannot be content with the present level of Asean cooperation: Asean has a greater role to play in international relations and in promoting intra-Asean economic cooperation. Asean must proceed to a higher plane of cooperation, collective action and self-reliance in order to have an effective voice in international, interregional and multilateral fora.

It is only a strong and united Asean which can exert its collective weight and voice to ensure that justice, fair play and even-handedness continue to be the guiding principles in the construction of the new international political and economic order. It is only a strong and united Asean which can contribute towards shaping that new order.

While regional peace and security are essential preconditions for our economic growth, the new world order which we should strive for is not only one that is free from the threat of war but it should also be a world free from poverty, hunger and diseases as well as an order which promotes equal economic opportunity and easy access to modern technology for all countries and peoples. And, most important of all, it should be a world order which recognises that countries and peoples can and must be allowed to maximise their national political, economic and social potentials in ways compatible with their historical, cultural and national circumstances.

It is from a strong Asean base that we should approach the question of peace and security of our immediate wider environment in the Asia-Pacific region. Asean has already made its mark in terms of geo-politics. The relevance of Asean for our regional existence as well as in international affairs has been proven beyond doubt. It is equally important that we should make Asean relevant in terms of geostrategy. A new strategic environment is clearly developing in the Asia-Pacific region following the effective ending of super-power rivalry in the area, but the shape of new things to come is yet unclear. This is for the Asean countries to study and assess together so that an effective and positive Asean contribution to peace and security in the Asia-Pacific region can be made.

In Southeast Asia itself, it is time for Asean to consider how the non-Asean states of the region can now be brought into the regional mainstream. The ZOPFAN Declaration of 1971 was an acceptance on the part of all member states of Asean of certain basic principles of intraregional relations. The Declaration also provided the guiding principles for extra-regional interstate relations. The Treaty of Amity and Cooperation of 1976 elaborated on these principles and invited acceptance of them by others in the region. Regionalism in Southeast Asia has to be brought to a higher plane from the process of communication and consultation to that of conscious and organised interdependence between all the regional states. Just as Asean provides for politico-economic interdependence, I believe the relevant elements of ZOPFAN and the Treaty of Amity and Cooperation can provide the structured politico-security framework for that organised interdependence between all Southeast Asian states.

A rapid pace of economic development requires an environment of peace and security. For so long as the Cambodian problem remains unresolved, it will continue to affect the peace and security of the region. Much honest efforts have been made to find a durable solution. Urgent matters on the international economic agenda requires our full attention. A Cambodia continuing to be at war will not only mean unending misery and suffering for its people but also affect the progress of the region.

At a time when regionalism is beginning to assume new importance in international economic affairs, we cannot afford to have the continuing division and the separation of the Indochinese countries from the rest of Southeast Asia. A Cambodia mired in perpetual turmoil while the other parts of the region and the rest of the world passes them by is a possible scenario, but we wish to prevent that from happening. However, in order to enable them to integrate into the regional life, Cambodians must first find peace among themselves. We are therefore much encouraged by the unanimous election of His Royal Highness Prince Norodom Sihanouk as the President of the Supreme National Council. We are confident under his wise leadership, the Cambodian parties would be able to achieve national reconciliation and reach agreement of a comprehensive political settlement.

There is no doubt that in the area of political and diplomatic cooperation Asean has made an international impact. But our performance on the economic front requires substantial upgrading. For more than ten years now, Asean's collective energy has been concentrated on finding a solution to the Cambodian problem. While we should continue to persevere until a solution is found, it is timely to give proper attention to economic matters. We need to refocus our economic cooperation, both internal and external, on those crucial areas that really matter. There must be new initiatives and ideas to step up economic cooperation, to give our economic front sufficient leverage, as well as to consolidate and upgrade our present cooperation.

While Asean should not be a trading bloc and each Asean country must remain free to trade with other nations, increasing steps should be taken to increase regional integration. We should be bold enough to examine specific areas where there can be greater regional integration, as for instance intraregional trade.

Asean's experience in the last worldwide economic slowdown of 1985-1987 period was a painful one. But it was a lesson well learnt. It is imperative that Asean pools its resources and collectively create a conducive economic climate in the region for renewed and enhanced growth. An Asean supported by economic strength will have a stronger voice in international negotiations for fairer trade terms with the developed countries.

To-date our volume of intraregional trade and investments remains small. The volume of intra-Asean trade remains at a low 20 per cent of Asean's total trade despite an increase in the number of products under the Asean Preferential Trading Arrangement. We cannot continue with the piecemeal approach to trade liberalisation among ourselves. I support, therefore, the recent proposal made by Prime Minister Panyarachun Anand Panyarachun of Thailand that we work towards the establishment of an Asean Free Trade Area sometime by the turn of the century.

I see merit in establishing an Asean Free Trade Area although there are many structural factors that inhibit our economic integration, such as our different levels of economic development, our competing economies, our lack of industrial complementation and our frequently divergent perceptions of short and long-term benefits both for the individual nation and the region. I appreciate that these are hard issues and harder still to make the choices. But make them we must if Asean wishes to be counted as an economic force in her own right.

Our economies, having registered some of the fastest growth rates in the Asia-Pacific region, will continue to grow, perhaps at a slower rate in view of the poor international economic climate. The future of the international trading system may be uncertain, but we are quite certain that the Asean economies will grow from strength to strength. Therefore, the factors which inhibit integration will no longer be so formidable or even relevant by the first quarter of the 21st century. By then, the economic disparity between Asean member states will have narrowed considerably, external and internal markets for Asean products would have expanded thus making the problem of competing economies less relevant.

Much as we need vision and foresight to chart the direction for Asean's future growth, we need more the courage and collective will of all to set our objectives on course and the achievement of these objectives within a time frame. We should set our minds to achieve what is, after all, quite possible.

As a start and for which we are already doing, albeit not in the pace that we should, there is the urgent need to liberalise our trade substantially within the grouping. Trade liberalisation will not only bring our economic cooperation to a higher plane, it will also reinforce our trade links with other countries and regions. We should strengthen our political cooperation by economic means. There is much room to increase trade flows, to create a larger market for complementary industrial ventures, to encourage greater private sector participation and to widen as well as give more impetus to Asean industrial joint ventures.

Just as we ask our trading partners to heed our call for a fairer and equitable trade terms, we have to demonstrate positive efforts of our own. I am quite certain that a liberalised Asean trading area will be a source of strength for us in the wider multilateral trading environment.

When we advocate a more economically integrated Asean, no one should mistake it as an idea to make Asean a trading bloc. Far from it. The outward dependence and orientation of our economies make it impossible for us to be self-contained or inward-looking. It would be illogical for us to abandon the multilateral trading system under which Asean economies have prospered. Consistent with our dependence on the open international trading system and multilateralism, Asean cannot but defend and seek to preserve them.

Much has been said about the need to revamp the Asean Secretariat. There is now consensus to restructure and strengthen the Secretariat to enable it to step up programmes for intraregional as well as extra-regional economic cooperation. But consensus must readily be turned into reality. It is in Asean's interest to be innovative, to improve its coordination and to accelerate the process of decision-making in the light of rapid changes in global economic conditions. A strong and effective Secretariat is a necessity to bring about changes in the methods and increase in the substance of Asean economic cooperation. Your task is to determine how best the Asean institutional machinery and in particular the Asean Secretariat is to be improved bearing in mind the requirements of the Association in the future.

A strong and effective Asean Secretariat will pave the way towards making Asean more economically integrated. It is therefore essential that we work towards making Asean more viable and relevant in the next century. It will engender self-reliance and resilience, enabling Asean economies to sustain economic dynamism and to withstand economic crises.

16

Asean: Daunting Task to Cope With Information Volume

"The Asean Ministers responsible for Information face a daunting task. They have to be responsible for both the free flow of information as well as ensure the stability of their countries. There will be many occasions when the two seem incompatible, when their responsibility for the development of their countries seem to run counter to their faith in the freedom of democracy."

EVENTS appear to be moving very fast these days in all parts of the world—in Eastern Europe, in the Americas, in Africa and in Asia and, of course, in our own neighbourhood. These events will invariably affect the course of history—for better or for worse. With the advances in all fields of communication

---

A speech delivered at the 2nd Conference of Asean Ministers for Information in Kuala Lumpur, Malaysia, on August 1, 1991

the world has now become a global village and consequently thoughts or words or deeds reach the ears and even the eyes of everyone as frequently as they happen. We were able to sit in our houses and watch modern warfare being conducted on a real time basis. And countries can no longer shield their people from the happenings in other parts of the world. One of the most astounding results was the exposure of the failure of the ideology which led to it being abandoned in Russia and Eastern Europe.

There can be no doubt that the advances in communication technology have been largely beneficial to the human race. Their scope of awareness of the world they live in has been vastly enlarged. Far away places with strange sounding names seem no longer far or strange. Knowledge which had taken a whole lifetime to acquire in the past can now be learnt in an hour. There is a great deal more transparency in the affairs of man and of nations. Distance no longer separate, for the pressing of a few buttons will bring people within talking distance of each other.

Along with all these advances there is an explosion in the media industry, particularly the electronic media. The volume of information that is disseminated cannot be coped by any individual or society or nation. There are far too much news that are fit to print or to broadcast. Accordingly news must be chopped into digestible bits, interpreted, vetted, censored, analysed, and underlined by people in the information business, whether governmental or non-governmental.

What these people are doing are no doubt essential. Without proper presentation, news would be confusing and indigestible. Some people must therefore condense and vet what the people should read and what they should not. And these people, whether they be from the government or from the non-government organisations, must acquire a considerable degree of power. And power, they say, corrupts.

Freedom of the press is now accepted as an essential part of democracy. Quite rightly the dissemination of news by the press should not be suppressed. Governments have been able to subjugate their people by denying news. To allow governments to control the press is synonymous with totalitarian rule. Any government which interferes with the dissemination of news must therefore be regarded as undemocratic, a heretic in a world that now unanimously accepts democracy as an article of faith.

Knowing how powerful is the influence of information on the mind and action of people, and knowing also that it is impossible to distribute all the news as they happen and equally impossible for people to absorb all the news that is distributed, it is inevitable that the people involved in the information industry should select some happenings to report and to exclude the others.

In addition, it has now been accepted that the presentation of the news is also the right of those in the non-governmental information industry. Now we know that the narration of history by different people and different countries differ greatly. In history it is always the other country which is wrong. One's own country is always right. And so whole generations grow up to hate and despise certain countries because of what their history books narrate. The same can happen in daily reporting by the press. A distorted view of events can always be spread because the people in the press, like the national historians, have certain views.

But, of late, it has even been accepted that lies can be fabricated in the name of freedom of the press. With the increasingly powerful weapons at the disposal of the press, it is entirely possible for the press not only to create totally erroneous views and opinions, but actually to undermine the stability and even the economy of countries. And events have shown that the guardians and practitioners of press freedom are not averse to using this unlimited license. New and more telling ways are continuously being invented so that lies can be accepted as the truth.

During World War II, Dr Joseph Goebbels of Nazi Germany perfected the art of the half-truth as a means to consolidate the support of the German people, first for the Nazi Party and then for the territorial ambition of Germany. Today, we wonder how the highly cultured and humane Germans could perpetrate the horrors of Bergen-Belsen and Auschwitz, gassing and killing Jews and then glorying in their brutality. The answer lies in the effectiveness of Dr Goebbels propaganda machine. Even the most gentle Germans can be made into a beast if fed the kind of selected information that was cooked up by Dr Goebbels propaganda machine.

We do not have a Dr Goebbels anywhere now. But when the world community accepts that press freedom confers the right to fabricate and tell lies, then we are condoning at least a part of the practices of Dr Goebbels. The result may not be the brutes who terrorised Nazi Germany but certainly there would be people sufficiently prejudiced as not to be able to see anything right about others.

Another effect of a shrinking world and instant news is the evolution of a world press. Language is a very important factor in the world press. Obviously a newspaper circulated worldwide, say in the Mongolian language, if the Mongolian people have the kind of money to do this, is not going to have much impact on public opinion in the world. To be effective, the language must be one that is understood by the most number of people in the world. And the language is English, the national tongue of some of the most populous and richest countries in the world. It is not surprising therefore that the English-speaking nations largely control the world press. The non-English-speaking nations which are also poor cannot have access to the world press to give their views or versions of whatever news are reported about them.

As a consequence, the poor non-English-speaking nations feel naked and defenceless. If freedom of the press is to be meaningful, then everyone should be able to present his side of the story. What we are seeing is a one-sided exercise of that freedom. Those who have no access to the world press have no freedom.

We talk so much about human rights, justice and fair play, etc. The question that must be asked is whether there is justice and fair play when only certain people can influence the minds of the world community, and whether human rights is not denied when whole nations are deprived of their right of expression and their freedom to air their views. Does press freedom refer only to the freedom of those who control the press in a country and not to the freedom of the people to air their views in the press? Does freedom of the press exist when only certain nations can air their versions of the truth and others may not?

Some years ago there was an attempt by poor countries to reform the international information order. Normally there is sympathy for the poor, but there was no sympathy shown to the poor nations' attempt to gain access to the international media and to fair reporting. One of the biggest United Nations agencies was threatened with a cut-off in its finances if it entertains the pleas of the poor nations. And so with unseemly haste the new information order was jettisoned. The right to fabricate, to tell lies and to do selective and slanted reporting about poor nations remains.

The Asean countries are a group of developing nations anxious to make as rapid a progress as possible towards a developed stage. Although by comparison the Asean countries have done quite well, as developing countries they have all the weaknesses associated with such a status. To develop they will need as little hindrance as possible.

One of the most important preconditions for them is political stability. This precondition can only be achieved if the people are well-informed, responsible, and aware of the results of their own action.

Democracy confers on the people rights and freedom of action. But rights and freedom are not free-standing entities. They must be accompanied by a sense of responsibility.

For a democracy to succeed the people must therefore be appreciative not only of their rights but also their responsibilities. This can only come about through a process of formal and informal education regarding democracy, which we all know is an alien concept.

It is in the area of informal education that information ministries, agencies and departments of governments have to play a big role. It is the duty of government to give some guidance without converting a democracy into a guided democracy. The line between merely guiding and being a guided democracy is difficult to draw. Too little guidance may result in irresponsibility, too much may negate democracy.

Yet the people must know that it is in their interest to be responsible in the exercise of democratic freedom. They must know that there is no monopoly by anyone in the definition and exercise of democracy. They must know that democracy is meant to serve the people. The exercise of democratic rights to the point where the people continuously suffer instability, insecurity and low or negative economic growth would seem to negate the objectives of being democratic. Yet, in most instances, it is not democracy which is at fault but the failure to understand it or worse still, the manipulation of democracy by self-serving people.

People who understand the way democracy works and its limitations will be able to derive the maximum benefit from the system. The mindless acceptance of someone else's interpretation of democracy and an unquestioning submission to certain practices, as for example the right to fabricate and tell lies, will undermine not only the fledgling democracies but the democratic system as well. This, the countries of Asean can ill-afford.

Governments have a duty not only to protect democracy and freedom, but also to bring about social and economic well-being for the citizens. While governments should not suppress the truth; while there should be press freedom and a free flow of information, governments would be failing in their duty if they allow abuse of press freedom to the extent that lies can be spread and the stability and economic well-being of the people undermined.

The Asean Ministers responsible for Information face a daunting task. They have to be responsible for both the free flow of information as well as ensure the stability of their countries. There will be many occasions when the two seem incompatible, when their responsibility for the development of their countries seem to run counter to their faith in the freedom of democracy. It is not easy for example to ban a newspaper or expel a journalist. You don't do such things without getting a bashing from the Fourth Estate and those who consider themselves holier than us.

Tolerance must therefore be stretched to the maximum. But no tolerance is necessary when there is evidence of deliberate lies which undermine the nation.

17

Asean in the 1990s and Beyond

"Asean came about because the Southeast Asian countries in the early days of their independence, faced many border problems. Claims and counterclaims and the eventual Confrontation by Indonesia against Malaysia had to be resolved. Military solutions were not successful. As a result an association of neighbours was formed to provide a forum for settling problems between members."

THE world has undergone truly radical changes in recent years. The collapse of the communist system and the ending of the great East-West divide led many to believe that we are all set to reap the peace dividend. But the Gulf War and the attempt of the hardliners in Russia to stage a coup

---

A speech delivered at the U.S. Council of Foreign Relations in New York, United States, on September 26, 1991

should remind us that dividends are not there for the picking but must be worked at.

There is a great need to understand the aspirations and sentiments of national, ethnic, social and political groups and the problems they must face when political changes take place. Above all there is a need to appreciate that different situations call for different remedies. The idea that there is one solution to all problems, and that what serves one situation should serve all situations must be discarded promptly if there is going to be any dividend at all from the peace we have apparently achieved.

Democracy and the free market have become the sole ideology and system for the world. Anything other than this is taboo. There is no real disagreement about accepting democracy or the free market. But while everyone agrees on the principle, the details are another matter. Democracy lends itself to many interpretations and reinterpretations. The advocates and practitioners of democracy in the West are wont to add new criteria for democracy which the newer practitioners are not quite ready for. But the new converts are not to be allowed to differ or defer.

Thus originally democracy simply meant majority rule. Everyone accepts that. But then minorities must have rights. This too is fairly reasonable. But now minority rights and even individual rights are to be regarded as more important than the rights of the majority. More than this, individuals from the senior democratic countries apparently must be accorded the right to break the law of other allegedly less democratic countries.

When Gorbachev started talking about perestroika and glasnost and indicated his desire to reduce tension between East and West there was a great deal of scepticism. But his subsequent action in releasing the Eastern European countries from Soviet military hegemony not only brought undisguised jubilation in the West but also among those countries which were the targets of communist subversion.

Today we all know that the process that Gorbachev started was not some communist trick but an earnest and total rejection of the communist ideology. We all have reason to celebrate, the West, the non-communist world and the peoples who had long been oppressed by communist rule.

In Southeast Asia, the countries which comprise Asean are glad to welcome the end of the Cold War. Without exception the six countries had all felt the full brunt of communist subversion and insurgency. It was only with great difficulty and debilitating cost that they all managed to overcome their insurgents even while they develop democratic systems with free-market economies.

With the end of the Cold War they fully expect to grow and prosper in a period of political stability.

The countries of Asean all rejected the kind of extreme and restrictive nationalism which elsewhere had hampered the development of newly-independent nations. Instead they opted to trade freely with the rest of the world and indeed to welcome foreign involvement in their economies. Where others restrict foreign investments, the Asean countries provided incentives to attract them.

They have a right to think that a world free of East-West confrontation would boost their trade and contribute towards faster economic development.

But what they see happening is not entirely what they had expected. They see doors being slowly closed.

They see funds being diverted away from them. They feel pressures being applied against them not by communist enemies but by democratic friends. They see, in fact, deliberate attempts being made by their perceived friends to stifle their growth and keep them forever at the state of developing nations.

The Asean countries are democratic. As colonies of the Western powers they were only familiar with the autocratic system of their colonial masters. Yet when they achieved independence they were expected to practise a democratic system of government with all the sophistications of the erstwhile democracies of the West. Shortcomings were promptly criticised as were failures to keep up with the latest in democratic concepts.

With populations which do not understand the workings and the limits of democratic freedom, with ethnic and regional divisions, with religious sensitivities, it is a wonder that any of the developing democracies survived at all. But a few did survive.

Those that survive should really be congratulated and given an occasional pat on the back by the established democracies. Despite their clumsiness with the democratic system some have not only survived but have actually developed economically. But instead they were harassed all the way.

They were harassed before the end of the Cold War. They are harassed even more now. It may sound like an exaggeration but for a developing country even the smallest obstacle is sufficient to retard development.

Today human rights, labour rights, extractions of timber, eating rice, minority rights, individual rights, death penalties, intellectual property, export processing zones and incentives and a host of other subjects are used to curb the growth of developing countries.

At one time countries which industrialised rapidly were classified as Newly Industrialised Countries (NICs). These countries were very happy to be so categorised until they found that being so classified involved withdrawal of trading privileges and impositions of measures such as currency revaluation, upward revision of workers' pay and scrutinising labour practices and human-rights records, all of which were calculated to retard the process towards developed nation status.

Only Japan got through, having caught the developed nations of the West napping. Clearly no other Eastern nations are going to be allowed to achieve developed status.

The four Asian NICs, in a way, caught the West unawares also. Now apparently any eastern nation must be stopped even earlier. And so the Asean nations like Thailand, Indonesia and Malaysia are already suspect although their per capita, one of the major criteria for classification as NIC, are less than half of the present NICs. Threats of reduction of loans, withdrawals of GSP rights, countervailing duties, reduction of quotas are already being heard. It would not be long before those threats are translated into deeds. The Asean countries, with the exception of Singapore, stand a real chance of becoming permanently developing countries.

The countries of Southeast Asia need trade much more than they need aid. They have all developed by utilising to the full the free international trading system. Their competitive advantage is their skilled and highly trainable labour force. With low cost of living and a low level of expectations, wages need not match those of developed countries for equivalent work.

The freedom to unionise and to strike may be the inalienable right of workers, but when jobs are scarce and strikes may reduce investments and make jobs even scarcer, it is questionable whether the exercise of the traditional rights of workers which reduces job opportunities will bring them a better life.

Yet workers in the developing countries of East and Southeast Asia are being instigated to demand for more pay and to disrupt production. Are their enthusiastic supporters in the developed countries trying to help them or to reduce the competitiveness of their products against the products of Western workers?

But as if this attempt to reduce the competitiveness of our exports is not enough, a whole series of other measures have been taken to stifle growth in the dynamic nations of Southeast and East Asia.

The freeing of the Eastern European countries from Russian hegemony is a welcome result of the collapse of communism. But it is clear that the Europeans and the Americans are much more sympathetic to the plight of their European kins and are ready to channel funds for their economic rehabilitations.

Of course we are assured that the countries of the South will continue to get funds. However, we all know that there is only so much money available and if some are diverted elsewhere then there will be less for those who before were the sole recipients. And because we know this we have a right to suspect that the assurances are hollow.

Then there is the European Community. Slowly but inexorably all the countries of Europe are being drawn into this exclusive club. There is every indication that the former Comecon countries will join the club as well.

By itself the enlarged European Community will be sufficiently big to be totally independent, economy-wise from the rest of the world. They would have all the raw materials and all the manufacturing technology to sustain their economic growth and well-being. With no threat of an East-West War they will need no allies outside their community. A Fortress Europe is not a far-fetched idea. It is a distinct possibility. Asians may be kept out of the European market.

Perhaps this is too pessimistic a picture. But in business we always have a worse case scenario. And if Asean nations think of this scenario, they cannot be condemned for being alarmist. After all when we predict a worse case scenario we know some part of it is likely to come true. And even some part can do a lot of damage. Certainly a Fortress Europe will damage the growth rate of Asean nations.

Then we have the NAFTA and the germ of an idea for an Enterprise of the Americas. We are told that NAFTA will not be a trade bloc and that the members would continue to trade with the rest of the world.

The U.S. is the biggest single market in the world. Malaysia's trade with the U.S. makes up 18 per cent of its total trade. While some Malaysian manufacturers enjoy GSP status, others compete unaided in the U.S.'s markets. On the other hand, some products, such as palm oil, are actually discriminated against. The other Asean countries have nearly the same trade relations with the U.S.

What NAFTA does is to let Mexico enjoy unrestricted and tax-free access into the U.S. Mexico is a developing country with a huge low-cost labour force. Mexican tax-free goods should enjoy competitive advantage against similar goods coming from distant Southeast Asian countries. Attracted by this advantage, American manufacturers have already invested in Mexico. Soon the Japanese and the Taiwanese will be investing in all kinds of manufacturing facilities in Mexico.

We wish Mexico well. But investments by American, Japanese, Taiwanese and possibly the Europeans in Mexico will divert much needed funds from Southeast Asia. Worse still what Mexico produces for the U.S.'s market would be cheaper and more competitive than what the Southeast Asian countries can produce. Imports into the U.S. and Canada from Mexico would cut into the export earnings of Southeast Asian countries, even if they still get GSP status.

Now consider the Enterprise of the Americas. If the privileges of the NAFTA are extended to all the Central and South American countries, not only will the Americas be self-contained and independent of all resources and products from the rest of the world but the bloc can use its economic strength to bludgeon the non-E.C. countries into economic submission.

Again this may sound too exaggerated. The U.S. and Canada would not want to do this. But in many instances the U.S., in subtle and not so subtle ways, have already been doing a lot of economic armtwisting.

The U.S. have threatened to limit imports or apply countervailing duties or penalise countries for anything that the U.S. unilaterally decide as infringements of the many regulations that govern trade with the U.S. Trade is restricted severely until countries sign the protection of intellectual property agreements. Countries are put on the "Watch List" which is not different from criminals being put under surveillance. GSP privileges are examined every year as are the quotas on imports, a practice that creates uncertainty and discourages investments in productive facilities.

Unrelated to trade, yet indicative of the attitude of the U.S. towards international laws and norms is the arrest of the leader of a country through military action and then charging him under the U.S. laws in the U.S. courts. This is the first extraterritorial enforcement of a national law. If a country is willing to ignore world opinion, what guarantee is there that it will not, when it becomes the sole world power, do what it likes in order to protect what it considers as its own interests.

If the countries of Asean feel that the international marketplace is about to be divided between the great economic entities and closed to them, can they really be blamed?

Asean cooperation in the economic field is minimal. But the performance of Asean countries in developing themselves is not unconnected with their regional cooperation.

The Association has helped to stabilise the region politically and militarily. It is this atmosphere of regional peace and stability which enables the Asean nations to develop. While intra-Asean trade is minimal and contributes little to the members' economies, learning from each other the skills of economic and development management has helped them grow rapidly. The Asean formula for growth is identical. That is why all Asean countries have open markets, welcome foreign investments and look towards an export led growth.

This last strategy is important and is the cause of their fear and anxiety over the trend towards the setting up of *de facto* trade blocs in Europe and America. Clearly they have to do something about it.

Asean can expand. Right from the beginning Asean was meant for all Southeast Asian countries. Obviously the Indochinese countries and Myanmar are geographically eligible. So far they have not been invited for obvious political reasons as well as the fact that they are not open free-market economies.

The ease with which Brunei was admitted is indicative of the openness of Asean. It is most likely that Asean will welcome Vietnam, Cambodia and Laos in the near future. All three countries are beginning to appreciate the benefits of a free-market system or at least the importance of national development over territorial acquisition.

The Vietnamese leaders have been visiting the Asean countries and it is unlikely that they failed to notice the prosperity of these countries. That they have noticed is evidenced by their request for information on banking and administration in these countries. They have asked for foreign investments although from selected countries at the moment.

Still it must be remembered that Asean is not an economic community. Asean came about because the Southeast Asian countries in the early days of their independence, faced many border problems. Claims and counterclaims and the eventual Confrontation by Indonesia against Malaysia had to be resolved. Military solutions were not successful. As a result an association of neighbours was formed to provide a forum for settling problems between members. Asean is therefore more a political grouping than an economic grouping.

Politically there is a need for Asean to establish good relations with the Indochinese states in order to ensure regional stability. For this reason alone Asean would welcome membership of the Association by the Indochinese states. The Prime Minister of Thailand has already openly welcomed membership by the Indochinese states.

Papua New Guinea has already been accorded observer status. Sri Lanka has expressed interest to join. Possibly Myanmar might get interested.

So expansions of Asean are in the cards. But what would be the benefit of enlarging the membership of Asean? It will be noted that the potential new members are weak economically. The combined economic strength and political influence of the enlarged Asean is unlikely to be improved. If in fact the trade blocs of Europe and America become inward looking, the Asean group is unlikely to be able to prise open the rich markets on which their economy depends. Indeed they may not even enhance their influence in the trade negotiations in the GATT.

Consequently Asean needs to enlarge its circle of friends if not its membership. In the Far East there are a number of dynamic countries which can help amplify the voice of Asean. These are China, Taiwan, Hong Kong, South Korea and Japan.

These countries are also very dependent on world trade and the free market. It would be in their interest to add their voices to those of Asean. The proposed East Asian Economic Grouping (EAEG) would bring the Asean countries, the potential members and the dynamic economies of East Asia together. This will not be a trade bloc for the simple reason that their economies largely compete with each other and trade between them is a very small proportion of their total trade. The usefulness of the EAEG lies in the strength of their combined voice in the GATT rounds in particular and in international trade negotiations, in general. A forum of East Asian countries is all they need for this.

All these countries are expected to vote for free trade with as few conditionalities as possible. Their combined economic strength will lend weight to their views. Of course a self-sufficient Europe and the Enterprise of the Americas can still ignore the EAEG. But the EAEG combined market will be too attractive for Europe and America not to negotiate with.

Assuming the worse scenario again, i.e., Europe and America do not care, the East Asian market can support the members of the Group to a considerable extent. Investment in each other's country, using the considerable technologies and marketing skills that they have, can stimulate East Asian growth sufficiently. Certainly by learning from each other as the Asean countries have done, the chances of their achieving high growth rates are good. And if they should grow in a world divided into trade blocs, the imperatives of growth will eventually force the trade blocs to open up and free trade will be restored.

The U.S. oppose the EAEG and are known to apply pressure on various countries including members of Asean. Vice President Dan Quayle was reported to have said that there should be no grouping in the Asia-Pacific region which does not include the U.S. Obviously the U.S. can be members of NAFTA and any Pacific grouping but East Asians may not even talk to each other.

The U.S. is especially concerned that Japan does not join the EAEG. The U.S. feel that this will allow Japan to dominate East Asia economically and politically. The Greater East Asia Co-Prosperity Sphere touted by Japan in the last war was resuscitated to frighten East Asians of the possibility of Japanese hegemony.

I think East Asians are mature enough to think for themselves. The stand of the U.S. suggests a desire on the part of this great nation to exercise hegemony over East Asia. We think of the U.S. as a friendly country but domination by a friend is no more welcome than domination by an enemy.

If East Asians are not afraid of Japan, why should the U.S. worry about it? The U.S. is the most powerful nation in the world. Modern Japan, on the other hand, has gained more through trading with the world than through war. It is unlikely for Japan to exchange the economic approach for the dubious chances of military adventures.

More likely the U.S.'s stand is due to a desire to prevent Asian countries from achieving developed status through working together. If one does not know better one would say there is a racist element in this attitude. But, of course, the U.S. has a proven record of being racially liberal.

Malaysia and Asean will press on for the formation of the EAEG. We assure you that we have no intention of becoming a trade bloc or to commit economic suicide. As nations and as peoples we have a right to associate with whoever we like and to develop. If the West cares for human rights then do not deny us the right to progress to the level of the Caucasian Europeans. If we are denied this while the East Europeans are helped to achieve developed status then we must conclude that colour and race still influence the thinking of the West.

18

Asean Should Study the Benefits of the East Asian Economic Grouping (EAEG)

"If Asean is to have a bigger say in trade negotiation internationally, then it must work together with the East Asian countries. The East Asian Economic Grouping (EAEG) will be sufficiently strong to gain the respect of both the E.C. and the NAFTA."

NEXT year the 4th Asean Summit will be held and Asean leaders will again be reviewing the progress achieved and so plan new directions for the future. Unfortunately, the record of achievements, particularly in the field of economic cooperation, has been dismal. This AEM meeting must, therefore, come out with bold and concrete recommendations to the Asean leaders that will push Asean economic

---

A speech delivered at the Meeting of Asean Economic Ministers (AEM) in Kuala Lumpur, Malaysia, on October 7, 1991

cooperation forward and fast. This is crucial if Asean is to survive as a viable organisation in view of the dramatic changes that are occurring worldwide.

The political and economic scenario of the world under which Asean existed in the 1970s and 1980s has been radically transformed. The socialist-command economies of Eastern Europe have collapsed and are being replaced by a free-market system. The Soviet Union is undergoing a political and economic upheaval of unprecedented proportions which will move it away from the rigid centrally planned economies of the past to a more market oriented system. China has been opening up her economy to world trade and investments for the past decade and has fairly successfully juxtaposed a free-market system with a centrally planned economy. There is no doubt that China today is economically healthier than the China of the Cultural Revolution and Maoism.

Elsewhere the trend is the same. Countries are steadily discarding ideologies and structures based on state monopolies and protection which had failed to generate economic growth and improve their people's standard of living, in favour of more liberal open-market policies and the active participation of the private sector. This is evident in Latin America, parts of Africa and Asia.

The Asean countries have always been free marketeers. The rapid economic growth of Asean members since their independence is testimony to the effectiveness of a free economic and trading environment. However, it is important to remember that the mere espousal of free trade and democracy will not generate economic growth or equitable wealth distribution. We are seeing now the early failures of the free market and democracy in the former countries.

Indeed, their situation now is worse than when their economies were centrally planned. To succeed, the people must understand the limits of democratic freedom and the skills of entrepreneurship and management necessary for the free-market system to deliver results. Additionally, free trade will not succeed if the trading partners practice protectionism.

It is ironical that while we have adopted the liberal economic policies based on free and open markets recommended by the West, they are now forming trade blocs which would effectively restrict entry of our products into their markets. The failure of the GATT talks and the Uruguay Rounds is due to the erstwhile free traders abandoning free trade and opting for managed trade. Trade blocs are being formed, by whatever name they may be called. Tariff and non-tariff barriers are being openly erected. Left unchecked there is a very real danger that international trade will not only be restricted, but will be restricted by those countries most capable of restricting trade.

It is therefore in the interest of the world economy that the Uruguay Rounds is brought to a successful conclusion. Asean and other countries which believe in free trade must use whatever influence they have on the developed countries, in order that they will continue their commitment towards the success of the Rounds.

The reality of the situation is that the Asean countries are dependent on exports to the developed countries for their growth. If the developed countries close their markets, then Asean economic growth will be retarded. It is imperative that Asean countries cooperate closely in order to ensure that free trade continues. But Asean by itself is not strong enough to protect free trade. Its combined market is only one-tenth of the market of the NAFTA countries or the single European market.

If Asean is to have a bigger say in trade negotiation internationally, then it must work together with the East Asian countries. The East Asian Economic Grouping (EAEG) will be sufficiently strong to gain the respect of both the E.C. and the NAFTA. Even presently the countries of Southeast and East Asia together form a formidable market. But the potential for growth of the EAEG is far greater than that of the E.C. and NAFTA. This fact will also increase the clout of the EAEG.

It is important that the EAEG should not be a trade bloc. All the countries of the group should be free to trade with anyone under GATT rules. But when it comes to negotiation to maintain a free trading system for the world then the group should meet to discuss issues and take a common stand. It would be very difficult for the trading blocs of Europe and America to ignore the common stand of the EAEG. Since the EAEG stands for free trade, its strong influence in the GATT rounds is likely to yield positive results.

The Asean experience is that although our association is not basically economic, the members of the group are able to learn from each other the best way towards developing our countries. It is not an accident that of all the developing countries of the world, the Asean countries are the most consistently successful in development.

There will be members of the EAEG which will be economically weak. If the experience of Asean is anything to go by, these weak countries will learn from the mistakes and methods of the successful countries of the groups and will soon develop and prosper. And when they prosper they will become better markets for

Asean goods and so contribute towards Asean prosperity. Thus the EAEG will evolve into a very strong grouping able to influence trade negotiations in favour of free trade for the whole world.

Unless we have this group, Asean and everyone will be at the mercy of the trade blocs of Europe and America. There will be so many conditionalities and linkages with non-trade issues that the growth of Asean countries will be retarded. We will all remain developing countries forever.

I have been extolling the virtues of the East Asian Economic Grouping as an instrument to keep world trade free. We expect this meeting of Asean Economic Ministers to endorse fully the positive recommendations of the officials tasked with examining the concept. However, we will understand if consensual endorsement is not possible. Malaysia values its association and friendship with its Southeast Asian neighbours above everything else. It does not wish to be a cause of embarrassment to anyone.

While we strive for the formation of the EAEG we should continue to work on the liberalisation of the Asean market. Malaysia welcomes the proposal of the Prime Minister of Thailand for an Asean Free Trade Agreement. The potential for intra-Asean trade is big but we have to open up our markets if we are to realise this potential.

The economic liberalisation policies undertaken by Asean countries mean that the private sector must assume a greater role in promoting trade and economic cooperation. It is disappointing to note that the number of Asean joint ventures is still small despite the existence of the AIJV and the Brand-to-brand Complementation and the preference given to their products under the PTA. The Asean private sector must prepare itself to meet the challenges by fostering greater linkages and networking among themselves.

Asean industries must increase their efficiency and competitiveness in order to survive and prosper. They could not depend any longer on a closed and protected home market while Asean countries are striving to forge a bigger Asean market by reducing tariff and non-tariff barriers. They must be ready to face the challenges and the opportunities that will arise out of a greater Asean economic cooperation.

The world is already moving towards a globalised pattern of production in which locations and nationalities have given way to efficiency and competitive advantage. Asean, and particularly its private sector, cannot afford to remain parochial. It must exhibit drive and dynamism and be the prime mover for Asean's progress.

In business, economies of scale is most important. And economies of scale depend on markets. While the markets in each Asean country may be able to support some industries, there are other industries which can only be viable and competitive if the market is Asean-wide. For these industries the Asean countries must be prepared to share their markets. Duplication of such industries in every Asean country will only reduce viability and competitiveness. In the small and medium industries which play a supporting role to the major major industries.

It would be far better at the initial stage, at least, to allocate certain industries to each one of the Asean nations—whether major industries or SMIs. When the market in each country grows sufficiently that each country can have the particular industry and still be viable, then the country concerned should have that industry for itself.

All that I am saying is not new of course. It was the basic idea behind the AIJVs. But logic and reason and even economic sense do not always prevail. And so today the Asean countries are still very far from becoming an economic group. We are more successful in cooperating politically. However, we should persist. One day Asean may yet be an economic group.

Environmental issues have lately come to the fore to join other economic and trade issues which already burden Asean economies. I have spoken at length on these issues in other fora and have pointed out the dangers of using them as leverage in trade negotiations. This problem can only be solved by cooperation between developed and developing countries and not through confrontational campaigns by some groups.

We in Asean can no longer remain passive and indifferent to these campaigns hoping that they will, in time, fizzle away. They have assumed serious proportions and are being used to obstruct the economic growth of the developing countries. The particular NGOs have enormous resources and have the support of the so called 'free western media'. Asean must coordinate its efforts to counter these campaigns before they become more damaging to our economy. We can do this through a massive information campaign at the international level, and by adopting a common stand on environmental issues. This will, no doubt, involve financial back-ups, but the price for not doing it now will be much higher later.

It must be pointed out that we in Asean are not unconcerned about environmental pollution. We are very concerned but our capacities to deal with them are limited. The developed countries should have a more positive approach rather than threaten to use trade and aid as instruments to force us into doing those things which will retard the growth of our economy and the well-being of our people.

A case in point is the current forest fires which have cast a thick haze over our countries. Forest fires are more damaging than the controlled extraction of timber. Forest fires destroy everything, every species of trees and plants, animals and insects and whatever else that thrive in the tropical forests. Forests fires lay bare tens of thousands of acres of land which will be leached and washed into the rivers when the rains come. The people who either live in the forests or depend on it for their daily bowl of rice are rendered destitute; some losing their homes and even their lives. And when forests burn, tons of carbon dioxide and probably other noxious gases are released into the atmosphere. In other words, the pollution of the environment by fires in the tropical forests is far, far greater than that caused by the extraction of timber.

But whereas the whole western world is in an uproar over our extraction of tropical timber and threatens to boycott our produce and destroy our economies, there is not a squeak about the forest fires which periodically plague us. Perhaps it is because the haze does not spread to their countries. Perhaps it is because they cannot sound noble as they do when they champion the Penans.

Yet there is much that is positive that the rich countries of the North can do about our forest fires. They can mount emergency operations to put out the fires. They can fly in their massive fleets of water-bombers to dump water on the fires. They can provide heavy equipment and pay for the cutting and removal of trees to create fire-breaks. They can do massive cloud-seeding to create rain. Indeed, with their ingenuity and wealth, they can put out our fires as they extinguish the oil-well fires in Kuwait with such handsome profits. But as we all know none of these things is happening. There is not a word from the environmentalists of the North or their proxies here.

On this and other issues and attempts to link non-trade matters to trade, Asean must speak with one voice and put forth our case with vigour. Individually we will be victims of the global campaigns now being mounted to make us permanent developing countries. United we stand a reasonable chance. Allied with other neighbours our chances becomes even better.

Consonant with efforts to forge greater trade and economic cooperation, Asean should also look into areas of strengthening cooperation among its research institutions both in the scientific and social fields. I realise that this has already been done to some extent in certain areas but more can be done. Asean countries spent large sums of money each year on foreign consultants to conduct all sorts of studies while the same expertise are available within Asean at a fraction of the cost.

Research in commodities has been one of Asean's strengths given its importance to Asean's economies. While it is accepted that this is something that countries would be reluctant to share because of its economic implications, we cannot totally discount the possibilities of cooperation. A good example is the case of palm oil and coconut oil. Both these products are victims of a vicious campaign to discredit them by certain groups overseas. Through more sharing of information and coordination of efforts among the institutions and agencies in the countries concerned, campaigns such as these could perhaps be countered more effectively and at lower cost.

As Asean forges ahead with various programmes at economic and trade cooperation, we must not neglect the important role of the Asean Secretariat in these endeavours and indeed in the functioning of Asean as an organisation. It has been said that an organisation can only be as good and effective as the secretariat that supports it. There has to be a revamp of the Secretariat and also of the various Asean Committees to ensure that decisions are made expeditiously and implemented. As the thrust of Asean's activities will be in the economic field, this aspect will need to be emphasised and strengthened in any future reorganisation of the Asean structure.

It is now almost four years since the last Asean Summit was held in which various proposals were made to promote further Asean economic cooperation. Unfortunately, the pace of progress is still painfully slow. For various reasons Asean is still unable to overcome the hurdles that lay in the path of cooperation. We seem to lack the political courage needed to move ahead and implement cooperative projects that will benefit us in the long term. If Asean is to enter the 21st century as an economic and political force that will be respected by others, then we would have to take the painful decision now before events overtake us.

19

Asean Among the Most Successful of Regional Groupings

"It is not an accident that the Southeast Asian countries of the Asean group are among the most dynamic in the world. We have demonstrated that peaceful neighbourliness and cooperation and a willingness to help each other can contribute greatly towards rapid development."

THIS meeting is timely because Asean needs to consider appropriate responses to the profound changes that have taken place in the world since the last Asean Summit in Manila in 1987. The final disposition of the new global political and economic order is uncertain but we must ready ourselves for all

---

A speech delivered at the 4th Meeting of the Asean Heads of Government in Singapore on January 27, 1992

the possible mutations of this order. In Southeast Asia itself changes will take place, and the form of cooperation which will result must be such as to strengthen our region and keep it continuously dynamic.

With the Cambodian problem on the way to resolution Asean must now transform the adversarial stance which characterised Southeast Asia in the past into new constructive relationships. It is not an accident that the Southeast Asian countries of the Asean group are among the most dynamic in the world. We have demonstrated that peaceful neighbourliness and cooperation and a willingness to help each other can contribute greatly towards rapid development. It is therefore equally likely that if all the nations of Southeast Asia were to adopt this approach to neighbourly relations and economic development, then all will be equally prosperous. A prosperous region will command respect and influence.

Asean must therefore take the initiative to reorganise its relations with the Indochinese countries. We can begin by establishing close and positive relations with them both bilaterally and as a group. Should they wish to do so we should welcome them as members of the Asean Group subscribing to our Treaty of Amity and Cooperation. We should promote and foster the concept of a Zone of Peace, Freedom and Neutrality as well as a Nuclear-Free Zone. I hope that the greatest military power with the most efficient intelligence agency is wrong when it predicts the possibility of a "Gulf War" in East Asia which can only be deterred by its military presence. By now all the nations of East Asia should have learnt of the futility of wars of conquest of the Gulf variety. They should have found that economic development and trade with neighbours highly beneficial.

Poor neighbours are no asset to anyone. The problems of the poor are likely to spill over in the form of refugees, smuggling, black markets, etc. Poor countries are not good trading partners. Helping neighbours to become prosperous is therefore mutually beneficial. If Asean wishes to be stable and prosperous then it must help its neighbours to attain prosperity. Above all, it must eschew confrontation.

While we should not let our different political systems stand in the way of mutual cooperation, we cannot of course support oppressive regimes which are not concerned with the well-being of their own nationals. Without interfering in the internal affairs of independent nations we must still strive to ensure acceptable standards of good government. It is the height of arrogance to claim that only a particular system is right and just. It is equally arrogant to claim that there is only one system of government which is right and just. The fact is that even democracy can bring misery to a lot of people. This we see in the violence and deaths during elections and the frequent riotings and strikes which reduce the productivity of nations and perpetuate poverty.

We see today a democratically elected government systematically depriving its legitimate citizens of political rights, dispossessing them, terrorising and killing them and generally behaving like a rogue but being supported by other democracies simply because it is defined as democratic. The empty shelves and the hunger we see in the new democracies of the Commonwealth of Independent States (CIS) and Eastern Europe are yet another evidence of the imperfections of democracy. We must not miss the forest for the trees. Democracy is not the universal cure it is made out to be. To succeed there must be circumspection in the application of the democratic process. No one should be forced or hurried into a system that they are unfamiliar with.

On the international front, the creation of powerful economic groupings to advance regional interests have become a reality of the international economic life. International trade and other economic relations are increasingly being managed to protect the positions of the powerful trade blocs.

In a world where peoples and countries are organising themselves regionally, it should not be so wrong for East Asian countries to come together. East Asia is a geographical entity, as much as Europe or America are geographical entities. Indeed, so is Southeast Asia.

If Southeast Asia can form an association in order to derive mutual benefit and still remain compatible with being members of the Asia-Pacific organisations, is there any reason why the East Asian countries cannot form a mere caucus and coexist with other organisations in the Asia-Pacific region?

The Asean experience has shown that when countries in a region consult and cooperate and speak with one voice, their status and influence are enhanced. Other countries and groups would certainly not have dialogues regularly with each and everyone of us separately. But as a group they will and they do. And in the process we have gained and have consequently developed much faster than other individual countries of the region.

The East Asia Economic Caucus (EAEC) will not be any kind of trade or economic bloc but a Caucus, an informal getting together of nations in East Asia for the purpose of consultation and to seek consensus so as to speak with one voice at international trade conferences. And that is all. We do not understand why we are not allowed to speak with each other or even to call ourselves East Asians. Is this a foretaste of the new world order?

We need a strong Asean base to be better able to face new uncertainties in the wider Asia-Pacific environment as well as a rapidly changing world. When the Cold War was on, we all yearned to be free from this oppressive conflict and the proxy fights and divisions it spins off. We in the Asean region have a right to be more free now since it is our side which won. But it would seem that we are now less free. The evolving new world order is full of restrictions.

An issue of equal importance to all countries and requiring global cooperation concerns the management of the environment. Unfortunately, there is undue focus on the tropical forest and its role in renewing the supply of oxygen, the preservation of flora and fauna and the ecological balance.

The fact is that the rich 20 per cent of the global population accounts for 80 per cent of the greenhouse gas emissions. Thirty per cent of carbon dioxide emissions come from one industrial power alone. On the other hand, in the developing world, 1.5 billion people live in abject poverty. Their fate is ignored when what is often their principal source of income, the tropical forest products, are boycotted.

If forests can save the world from the greenhouse effect, then the stress should be on a massive regreening of the world. It must be remembered that at one time the world was almost completely covered by forests. The natural changes as well as the changes brought about by men destroyed most of this forest cover. With the wealth of the rich and the technology at their command it is entirely possible to plant and cover even desert areas with trees, including tropical hardwood timber. Controlled logging can go on but in a hundred years there will be three times the present tropical timberland.

One issue, totally ignored, is the fact that forest fires cause greater damage to the environment than controlled logging. Developing countries do not have the financial and technological capability to effectively handle forest fires which can rage for weeks and months. Certainly, more forests can be saved by preventing forest fires or putting them out quickly than by boycotting the export of tropical timber or advocating that forest dwellers remain in the forest, eating monkeys and suffering from all kinds of tropical diseases.

It is claimed that tropical forests are a common heritage of the world. We dispute this, for we have a better claim to our forests than those who claim to own Antarctica. But if the world is so concerned about depleting tropical forest and think they have a right to it then they should do something about forest fires in the tropics. Massive and valuable equipment are available all over the rich countries of the North. Most of them would be under-utilised when there are no fires. It would be a simple matter for an international organisation to be set up to catalogue all these resources and deploy them to the poor tropical countries whenever there is a forest fire. This is much more constructive than dramatising the acreage of tropical forest destroyed per day or how 300 Penans are being deprived of their million hectares of hunting ground.

While we dispute the claim that our forests belong to the whole world, we have always accepted that certain straits and sea-routes through our waters are international waterways. The best-known of these international waterways is the Straits of Malacca.

It was of little concern to the littoral states when the ships passing through the straits were small and infrequent and carry no significantly dangerous cargo. But now not only have the numbers multiplied many times, but their sizes have increased tremendously. In addition the cargo they carry is often dangerous; as for example the oil and chemical tankers.

Already we have had collisions and the spillage of oil onto the sea and on our shore. Not only is cleaning up costly but damage to our fishing industry and our tourist industry is considerable. It takes months for fishing to be lucrative again.

Now we have a new problem—piracy. The pirates are not after the cargo but the cash and valuables belonging to the crew. In the dark of the night they clamber on to the ship and tie up the crew while they pillage and rob. And when they leave, the crew members remain tied. For hours the ship will sail unguided. It may deviate from its course and it may collide with another vessel or run aground, causing all kinds of damage.

Whose responsibility is it to keep these international sea-lanes safe? The littoral states collect no dues. Nor are they rich. On the other hand, maritime patrols by sea and by air are expensive. The maintenance of equipment and personnel to fight spillage and other damages are equally costly.

If the world is fond of claiming rights then the world must also accept responsibility. It is time that the international community appreciate the problems and the dangers faced by littoral states. Is it too much to ask that those who use the passage and the maritime nations contribute towards the cost of keeping them free and safe?

Asean is without doubt the most successful of the regional groupings of developing countries. We came together initially because we had to have a forum to resolve border problems in the postcolonial period. We have not resolved all of these problems but at least we agree that the Asean way is that of consultation and negotiation.

Having come together we felt it could be beneficial to cooperate economically as well. Again, with our competing economies we have not been very successful. Still we must soldier on.

But in the meantime the world has changed radically. I shall not repeat here what these changes are. What is certain, however, is that we will be affected by the fallout. We can survive, I think. We can even prosper as a result of these changes. But it is up to us to design our response if we want to come out of these changes stronger and more prosperous. It will require all our ingenuity to do this. Asean must emerge from the restructuring of the world, freer and more resilient and better developed than ever.

20

U.S.-Asean Business Council Plays Pivotal Role

"There is an unfortunate tendency in the U.S. to link trade with non-trade issues such as human-rights issues, labour practices, the environment and economic policies. The result of scrutinising these issues is to stifle trade."

IT gives me great pleasure to address the U.S.-Asean Business Council today. The members of this Council have not only played a pivotal role in promoting trade and economic relations between the U.S. and the Asean countries, but more importantly have recognised the need to enhance the

---

A speech delivered at the U.S.-Asean Business Council Dinner in New York, United States, on September 3, 1993

momentum of this mutually-beneficial cooperation between the two regions.

I am gratified too that the present U.S. administration has shown a greater interest in East Asia, especially trade and economic relationship with the region. With U.S. external trade alone exceeding US$1 trillion last year, it is gratifying to note that in the past few years there has been a phenomenal growth in trade between the Pacific countries and the U.S. Exports to the Asean region alone have grown by almost 25 per cent.

To ensure that this momentum is sustained, it is crucial that we maintain those conditions that have fostered growth and continue to explore ways to reinforce such conditions. Of these, free and fair trade have obviously contributed a good share towards the growth of trade between the two regions.

It is essential that new political, security and economic considerations brought about by the end of the Cold War do not negatively impact on our trade relations. The U.S.'s role in promoting the economic and trade potential with the Asean region cannot be overstated.

I understand that the most encouraging facet in the U.S. economy has been the growth in its exports. The new emphasis on exports is, I believe, a contributing factor. The U.S. needs trading partners, and we in Malaysia understand the importance of this. When we achieved independence we did not get rid of foreign business interests. Instead we encouraged additional foreign investments from Japan, Western Europe, Taiwan and the U.S. This has reduced unemployment and made Malaysia prosperous. The investing countries not only gained from Malaysia's comparative advantage, but the prosperity of Malaysia makes it a good market for their products as well.

There is an unfortunate tendency in the U.S. to link trade with non-trade issues such as human-rights issues, labour practices, the environment and economic policies. The result of scrutinising these issues is to stifle trade.

It should be noted that developing countries are disadvantaged. Frequently they depend on one or two primary commodities for their foreign exchange earnings. If they go into manufacturing they are handicapped by the lack of technological know-how, capital, domestic market or even management expertise. About the only thing they have is low-cost labour. If this is taken away from them or nullified in some way, they will not be able to industrialise at all. If they don't grow and prosper, then they will not be able to buy the products of the sophisticated developed countries. By stifling their growth you will in fact deprive yourself of markets for your products.

During the Cold War years, many developing countries grew accustomed to getting preferential access for their goods to markets in North America and Europe. Clearly these privileges render them vulnerable to threats of withdrawal. Malaysia, as a developing country, has GSP privileges. For some years now there have been threats of withdrawal because of alleged restrictions on the freedom of association of workers in the electronics industry. Now it is well-known that even in the U.S. not all workers are unionised. In Malaysia where electronic manufacturing companies are of various sizes and enjoy different degrees of profitability, we prefer that they have in-house unions rather than national trade unions. Powerful national unions have been known to destroy the economy of even developed countries. And when the economy is destroyed it is the workers who suffer the most. On the other hand, in-house unions can do little harm as they affect only the respective company. Yet in-house unions are still able to protect the interest of workers. Clearly our labour policy is in the interest of the workers.

The attractiveness of Malaysia as an investment centre is partly due to good industrial relations. Such is the attractiveness of Malaysia's investment climate that huge labour-intensive industries have been set up resulting in full employment. With full employment wages have gone up. Clearly Malaysian workers are not losing anything because of the Malaysian labour laws and policies.

Foreign investment remains a vital ingredient of Malaysia's economic and technological development. We are particularly interested in investments in the manufacturing sector. Last year, for instance, the manufacturing sector contributed 28.9 per cent of Malaysia's Gross Domestic Product (GDP). Manufactured products accounted for nearly 70 per cent of Malaysia's export earnings. Electronic goods make up 48 per cent of these exports. The overall result of the economic policy and its management is a growth of 8 per cent per annum for the last five years.

Usually high economic growths are accompanied by high rates of inflation. In Malaysia's case the rate has remained low—ranging from 2 per cent to 4.7 per cent. In fact, despite continued high growth, the inflation rate has actually gone down. It is now 3.9 per cent, down from 4.7 per cent in 1992.

We are also politically stable and blessed with a young, trainable and disciplined workforce. Infrastructure is continually being upgraded and expanded. Telecommunications facilities, banking and other services are well above average for a developing country, and are continuously improving. The Asian Development Bank (ADB) recently reported that Malaysia's banking system is among the best in Southeast Asia.

With all these going for us, it is regrettable that with the exception of the petroleum and the electronics sector, there have been few notable investments by American businesses. We continue to get far more investments from Japan, South Korea, Taiwan and Singapore than from the U.S. It is our desire to encourage and see more investments from the U.S., especially from the small and medium-scale industries.

The U.S.-Asean Business Council is aware of the vast opportunities that exist in the manufacturing sector in Malaysia. However, some of its members may not be aware of the opportunities in resource-based industries, agro-based industries, ancillary and supporting industries, the manufacturing of precision products and the manufacturing of industrial machinery and parts.

U.S. business is also welcome to set up regional operational headquarters in Malaysia. Foreign-owned multinational subsidiaries carrying out certain activities are provided with tax incentives. Labuan, an international offshore financial centre, also offers a number of business opportunities typical of tax havens. Foreign business may also come in and participate in activities associated with tourism and tourism-related projects.

I have outlined these broad parameters of business opportunities and the incentives for such activities to demonstrate our policy of welcoming foreign business investments.

Malaysia, like other developing countries, is also concerned that environmental conditionalities are being imposed to restrict the inflow of development funds from multilateral lending institutions and the export of certain finished products made from tropical timber. We have enacted laws to check illegal logging and bring down the annual harvest of tropical timber. Malaysia wishes to preserve its rainforests. It is in Malaysia's interest to do so. More than 50 per cent of Malaysia is covered by forests and if we include tree plantations, more that 70 per cent is tree-covered. We cannot be having 50 per cent forest cover if we are indiscriminate about logging.

Also, there have been reports that Malaysia and other countries in the region are involved in an arms race. The alarming tone of these reports conveys the impression that we live in mutual antagonism and discord among the countries of the Southeast Asian region. Southeast Asia is getting more prosperous and it is natural that we expand some money to upgrade our modest defence establishment. That is not an arms race. We believe in the negotiating table even with China. We do not look upon China as a potential enemy.

With the ending of the Cold War there is a tendency to believe that democracy has triumphed. To a limited extent the western democrats are right. But democracy does not mean the same thing to different people. Even among erstwhile western democrats interpretations differ. Unfortunately, some democrats do not believe in democracy when foisting that political system on others. They are quick to apply pressures and to make threats.

Democracy is not the easiest of political systems. It took the West several centuries to apply it. Even then it does not always work. Racial intolerance, fascism and unstable as well as ineffective governments abound. Italy is a good example. It is unrealistic to expect countries with no experience of the democratic system to suddenly espouse and excel as democracies. And the former colonial territories were never ruled through the democratic system. How are they to practise all the minute provisions of the latest western interpretation of democracy? Look at the bungling and near anarchy now bedevilling the countries of Eastern Europe and the former Soviet Republics. Indeed, the tragedies of Yugoslavia and others are directly attributable to the attempts at democracy.

Though disadvantaged in many ways, the developing countries aspire to develop their economies, uplift their peoples, and also provide some form of democracy in their political system. In the short term, the concerns of most countries are to provide food, shelter and clothing. In many countries, the pursuit of these objectives has been affected by a lack of political stability, ethnic and religious strifes, disunity and most frequently a lack of indigenous resources. Malaysia, fortunately, does not suffer from these disabilities.

Malaysia's development policies emphasise national unity, income redistribution, the eradication of poverty and the elimination of the identification of race with occupation. Our strategy combines economic, social, legal, labour and educational tools. We cannot allow criticisms of our laws and policies by outsiders to disorientate and destabilise us. To become dynamic, vibrant and prosperous we have to shape our policies and style of administration to our local situation—that of a multiracial developing country with very few resources initially.

Malaysia welcomes foreign involvement in its economy ever since it gained independence. That attitude and policy have paid off. We wish to continue with them. All we ask is some understanding and sympathy for our system and policies.

Americans, and in particular American businessmen, at least those who have been there, are sympathetic. But many Americans shape their opinions and act on the basis of newspaper reports. These reports are sensational and unsympathetic. Even economic and business reports are more political in content. The result is a distorted view among their readers. In the case of businessmen, there is a reluctance to invest in Malaysia. This is one of the reasons why American investments lag behind those of other countries. This is a pity because those who have invested in Malaysia have reaped very considerable profits. Indeed, even when they are not doing well at home, their Malaysian operations are profitable. I hope the U.S.-Asean Business Council can help correct the distorted view of Malaysia and bring about not only greater friendship between the two countries but more American investments.

21

Trade and Culture Can Foster Greater Asean Unity

"Governments can provide the necessary political, security and infrastructure framework but at the end of the day it is the businessmen who have to exploit the commercial opportunities that abound in this region."

I WISH to thank the organisers, the Asean Institute, for inviting my wife and I, to this 3rd Asean Achievement Award tonight. To the winners, my heartiest congratulations to you. Your success tonight is a recognition of your contributions to your community specifically, and the region generally. The

---

A speech delivered at the 3rd Asean Achievement Award organised by the Asean Institute in Kuala Lumpur, Malaysia, on July 22, 1994

initiative to honour outstanding individuals from the various disciplines, including medicine, architecture, Research and Development and education, is indeed commendable.

I understand that the Asean Institute is one of the largest regional private business organisations, dedicated to boosting Asean trade in addition to enhancing the cohesiveness of the Asean community.

We in Asean have enjoyed not only peace and stability but have also witnessed an era of strong economic growth throughout the region. Given these trends the next century could well go down in history as the golden age of Asean. However, for this to happen we must make concerted efforts to address a number of problems confronting us in the advancement of Asean as a strong and cohesive grouping.

While it is true that the economic performance of the individual Asean countries has been commendable many problems remain unresolved. Pockets of poverty are found in many Asean countries and positive actions must be taken to redress the imbalances between the haves and the many have-nots. In addition, more attention should be given to improving health care, and to raising the educational standards of our peoples. Without good health and education progress becomes difficult.

In fact, the premium placed on good education could not be over-emphasised. We must continue to invest in education in a world where new knowledge grows by geometrical progression. There is less need to go abroad now as our local educational institutions are more credible and they provide a wider range of courses to choose from. Asean countries should open up their educational institutions to each other.

Asean's success seems to draw some unwelcome attention. Efforts are being made to slow down its development through the imposition of foreign standards. Asean countries must stand together if they are going to counter this unhealthy move.

To build a cohesive Asean community, we need not focus on political or military alliances. Trade and cultural ties can be just as effective in fostering greater Asean solidarity. We should therefore work towards becoming economically and technologically a single community, i.e., sharing our expertise, experiences and thoughts so that the benefits could be shared between us.

The making of an Asean community is a matter which must receive more attention. Towards this end a variety of programmes, both social and educational, should be developed to forge closer ties between our countries. This is especially important among the youth of Asean, the people who will carry on the tradition and give substance to the Asean spirit. More exchange programmes between young people should be encouraged as this will provide them with a better insight into each other's way of life.

In this context, I am impressed by the Asean Business Forum which was created specifically as a private-sector initiative and that for the past three years it has been able to generate hundreds of millions of dollars as a result of new joint ventures between its members. This has definitely boosted intra-Asean trade.

I am also pleased to note that there are more than 40 Malaysian companies which are members of this Forum. As the private sector will always be the engine of growth it is imperative that it continually initiates ideas, innovations and approaches which can be commercially developed for the mutual benefit of entrepreneurs and consumers in the Asean region.

Governments can provide the necessary political, security and infrastructure framework but at the end of the day it is the businessmen who have to exploit the commercial opportunities that abound in this region.

I find it refreshing to note that the Forum, despite the strong emphasis on business activities, has included outstanding pre-university students at each of its annual banquets. These are but some of the strategies that must be followed through to ensure the success of our programme to train the young.

I find this exercise to honour individuals from the various disciplines a noble undertaking. That there is a group within Asean who are concerned with the young and who believes that students who excel in their respective discipline should be given regional and international recognition is indeed commendable. To provide motivation for the young to excel is one way to encourage professionalism.

Of all our resources, our greatest asset is said to be our people. But if people are to be assets for nations they must have skills, good values and a sense of responsibility. No nation can do well if the people are ill-educated and ill-trained and given to all kinds of disruptive activities. The development of a culture that is compatible with growth and development must be regarded as a priority for all Asean countries.

Our Asian values have been our strength and we should take all possible measures to ensure that these values are deeply ingrained in our society for generations to come. Without this strong sense of commitment to the community, family and nation, our efforts to catch up with the developed nation will end in failure.

We must relentlessly help to upgrade the well-being of our family, our community and our country. Collectively it will help to realise the Asean dream of a prosperous and peaceful Southeast Asia.

22

Enhancing Intra-Asean Investment in Agriculture

"The private sector of Asean countries can play a major role to enhance intra-Asean investment in the agriculture and forestry industry so as to exploit the complementarity within Asean in terms of factor endowments, labour costs, technologies, and skills. Asean private initiatives should aim at strategic alliances and joint ventures in the production, processing and marketing of agricultural products."

THE Asean economies today are booming and experiencing rapid economic growth averaging 6.7 per cent per annum in 1993. In all these economies, the leading sectors have always been the manufacturing and the services sector. Yet a large number of people are still highly dependent on

---

A speech delivered at the 16th Asean Ministers of Agriculture and Forestry Meeting in Langkawi, Kedah, Malaysia, on August 25, 1994

agriculture and forestry for their livelihood. The agricultural sector, compared to the manufacturing and services sector, has been lagging behind in terms of rate of growth and contribution to the GDP. As such efforts must be made to ensure that agriculture continues to develop alongside other sectors.

In Malaysia, between 1991 and June 1994, out of RM82.8 billion of capital investment that was approved for 20 types of industry, agro-based and food-based industries accounted for about 11 per cent or RM8.7 billion. This included food manufacturing, beverages and tobacco, wood and wood products, and paper and rubber products. Thus, even though the manufacturing sector takes on great importance in a country's industrialisation, the agriculture component is not an insignificant component. Besides, for Malaysia, the biggest import item and the biggest cause of inflation is food, especially imported food products.

The private sector of Asean countries can play a major role to enhance intra-Asean investment in the agriculture and forestry industry so as to exploit the complementarity within Asean in terms of factor endowments, labour costs, technologies, and skills. Asean private initiatives should aim at strategic alliances and joint ventures in the production, processing and marketing of agricultural products. The thrust of cooperative efforts in this direction should result in penetration of extra-Asean markets. With the conclusion of the GATT negotiations, there will be more trade and competition, and competitiveness will be the key to survival in the world marketplace. Hence all the comparative advantages of the Asean member countries should be combined in order for Asean to be a low-cost producer and exporter of quality agricultural products.

In Asean we have the Growth Triangle development strategy involving all Asean member countries, namely the IMT-GT between Indonesia, Malaysia and Thailand; the SIJORI between Singapore, Malaysia and Indonesia and BIMP-GT between Brunei, Indonesia, Malaysia and the Philippines. In all these projects, agriculture offers a great potential because these are resource frontier regions. I would, therefore, like to urge the private sectors of all the Asean member countries to initiate projects which would benefit all parties and help expedite the process of opening up these growth centres. Potential areas of development include food production and large-scale livestock rearing, as well as the various tree-crops.

We in Asean produce the same commodities, have the same climate, the same environment, eat the same staple food and face the same problems. In agriculture, as in other fields, we are both competitors and rivals. We want to be the best producers and to get the maximum market access for our products. In fact, we want to be the best in all our endeavours because entry into the world market means we can develop faster and improve the standard of living of our people. This is a logical and rational mode of thinking and action because the real world is a harsh one. But I believe we can do better if we cooperate rather than compete ferociously and fiercely. It is in this spirit that the Asean Ministers of Agriculture and Forestry (AMAF) meeting can play an important role. I hope that the AMAF will be an effective forum for the resolving of common problems related to agriculture and forestry in the region. We have no time to engage in polite and unproductive forums using scarce public funds that need to be used for the benefit of our peoples. We have to make a commitment to come up with more task-oriented and substantive work programmes. If we all do this sincerely and with commitment, then agriculture will continue to be an important contributor to our growth.

Although environmental issues have dominated the world scene since the UNCED summit held in Rio de Janeiro in 1992 the role of agriculture cannot be ignored. It is obvious that expansion of agricultural land must be at the expense of forest land. But we can minimise this by more intensive cultivation of available land and through research on increasing yield per unit of land. It is worth noting that research has made the original rubber tree yield ten times more latex. The same is true for oil palm and other crops. Still there are many ways of improving quality and yield. It is up to the agriculturists to do research and to develop. Funds expanded on R&D in agriculture is never a waste. Asean researchers should publish their works and exchange information on a regular basis. That way we can help sustain our environment and in particular our forests.

Growth in population tend to exhaust marine products. While fishing should be controlled, aquaculture should be expanded. Many Asean countries have more than adequate land for aquaculture. At the same time research in aquaculture should not only make the industry profitable but should help with the food needs of Asean countries, and for exports.

Asean remains a major tropical forest region in the world, with some 180 million hectares which represent about 60 per cent of the Asean land area. Asean is also the most important supplier of tropical timber products in the world, accounting for more than 80 per cent of the international trade in these products valued at more than US$12 billion a year. Forestry has played a dominant role in the socioeconomic development of the region.

You may recall that when the need to conserve the world's forests was first recognised, the focus was almost exclusively on the tropical forest and its exploitation. A full-scale and emotive campaign was mounted in the West to ban the use of tropical hardwoods. It would seem that temperate land timber has no role at all in maintaining the ecological balance. The timber tycoons of the north could clear-fell millions of hectare of forest with impunity.

While we are not denying the role played by tropical forests in sustaining the ecological balance, we would like to point out that we do no clear felling. Extraction of timber is controlled so that if you fly over the Asean countries, you will still see only green below you.

When Asean timber companies expand their operations to the South Seas and other regions they are equally careful not to destroy the forests they log. Unfortunately, the activities of Asean loggers to help the economy of many developing countries have aroused resentment on the part of some regional powers. Suddenly money was offered to these developing countries to persuade them to stop Malaysian investors. We do not know what to call such aid but it is questionable whether ecology has anything to do with it.

While many Asean countries can afford to reduce dependence on the forest for their economic development, other countries may not be able to do so. They have a right to extract their forest products in order to free themselves from others.

Finally, I am glad to note that the Asean Secretariat has drafted a Memorandum of Understanding for the Joint Asean Agriculture and Forestry Product Promotion Scheme in order to strengthen the collective bargaining position of Asean and expand agriculture and forest products exports. This MOU is very timely and in fact is long overdue in the quest for Asean economic cooperation in the face of a more competitive world economy.

On that note, I have the pleasure to declare open the 16th Asean Ministers of Agriculture and Forestry Meeting.

23

Asean Proves Regional Cooperation Beneficial

" There cannot be any doubt that membership of the Asean grouping has contributed towards governmental rationality and serious concern for the well-being and rapid development of member states. The members seem to learn from each other how to administer and develop their countries. They all seem to believe in working for the good of their people, even if their individual styles may differ."

YESTERDAY, we witnessed the official admission of Laos and Myanmar into Asean. We are therefore very close now to fulfilling the vision of the Founding Nations of Asean in 1967 to bring together all the ten Southeast Asian countries into one regional grouping.

A speech delivered at the 30th Asean Ministerial Meeting in Petaling Jaya, Malaysia, on July 24, 1997

While this vision is yet to be fulfilled, nevertheless the addition of Myanmar and Laos is a major milestone in the history of Southeast Asia. Malaysia feels honoured to be the host to this momentous event. Let me take this opportunity to congratulate and welcome our friends from Laos and Myanmar into the Asean community of nations.

We still have cause to celebrate but let us not forget the difficulties faced by the countries of Southeast Asia in their early attempts to form a regional forum, essentially to facilitate problem solving between newly independent neighbours. After two false starts, five of the Southeast Asian countries managed to launch Asean. It was political necessity rather than economic imperatives which brought these countries together. But almost immediately there was talk about these countries emulating the European Economic Community by becoming a trade bloc.

The level of economic development of these countries was very low then. An Asean economic bloc would have been quite meaningless. Besides, the claims over each other's territories remained to strain relations between various pairs of Asean countries. It is a measure of the pragmatism of these countries that they continued to meet as Asean, even though bilateral relations between certain members were strained. To this day the claims remain but they have not prevented Asean from developing into a regional forum with credibility in the world's economic, social and political affairs. Such has been the initial Asean-5's success that the other countries of Southeast Asia and even those outside evinced a keen desire to join it.

Asean's accomplishments are even more remarkable considering that not so long ago there were wars and conflicts in the region and within many of the

Asean countries. It was predicted that if North Vietnam achieved victory, then, like dominoes one by one the other countries in the region would fall to communism and chaos. We were told then, as we are told now, that we needed foreign protection against predatory neighbours such as a victorious Vietnam and the other powerful Eastern countries.

Against all odds Vietnam and its much derided soldiers in black pyjamas won against the greatest power on earth. But the dominoes did not fall. Instead, they prospered and showed themselves very stable and capable of managing their countries well. They seem prepared to shed the ideological baggage of the past and accept the need for economic reforms in order to give their people a better life. Central planning gave way to market forces and the promotion of international trade and foreign investments. Aggressive territorial acquisition appears to be the last thing on the minds of Southeast Asian leaders. Peace and good neighbourliness seem to be the preferred creed. And all evinced a desire to work together to build a nuclear weapons-free region of peace, freedom and neutrality.

There cannot be any doubt that membership of the Asean grouping has contributed towards governmental rationality and serious concern for the well-being and rapid development of member states. The members seem to learn from each other how to administer and develop their countries. They all seem to believe in working for the good of their people, even if their individual styles may differ. Asean has proven that regional cooperation among developing countries is possible and can produce results.

Very recently the World Bank has acknowledged that good government is the key to the development of poor economies. Conversely, it must be concluded that the poor economies which have now developed are blessed with good government.

The Asean countries have all been poor but are today among the most dynamic economies of the world. It follows that the governments of Asean countries know what is meant by good government and their model should be emulated.

The world should conclude that membership of Asean would have a steadying influence on domestic politics and would help the progress of member countries. The world should welcome the accession to Asean of any country which qualifies. It is regrettable that there are those who would not see the obvious. Instead of encouraging Asean to accept all Southeast Asian countries as soon as possible, Asean has been urged to pass judgement, deny membership and apply pressure on a potential candidate so as to force that country to remain poor and therefore unstable. Asean must resist and reject such attempts at coercion. They are not a part of the Asean way. We will resolve our problem in our own way and in our own time. No one, but no one should assume that only they know the solutions to all problems. They have failed far too often for us to be convinced that only they know what is right and what is wrong.

The countries of Asean, like all countries, need security and peace. We have decided that Asean will not become a military alliance in order to protect ourselves, although each one of us is free to have bilateral arrangements with other members for mutual security. Those who are concerned about our safety should support our concept of a Nuclear-Free Zone of Peace, Freedom and Neutrality. We see no enemy and we would not want to label anyone as our potential enemy. If we have problems with non-Asean countries, we will together seek a solution through negotiations using our unity as a lever.

We appreciate the offer to defend us but how can we be sure the promised help will be forthcoming when we see so many countries being abandoned to their fates as soon as they were in trouble. We know that the first priority of the protectors would be to pull out their forces. The pledge to protect human rights irrespective of borders and sovereignty has proven empty time and time again. We know we will be left to face the problem and to pay the cost with our lives and our wealth. In the final analysis we can rely only on ourselves. Forswearing force as a means of settling problems between ourselves, we can ensure our safety through a willingness to settle problems the Asean way.

For us, our ultimate defence will be our stability and economic strength as well as our willingness to stay together, even though we made no promise to fight alongside each other, not being a military bloc.

Economic strength is all-important. In a world dedicated to economic growth through a free-market system, territorial acquisition is no longer worthwhile. It is no longer a source of wealth and power. Those who talk of military conquests and colonial territories are living in the past. They know very well that other forms of hegemony is possible. The threat faced by nations is economic sanctions to impoverish the people and to stir internal strife. Weakened, the unfortunate countries will have to submit as completely as if they are colonies. We should therefore concentrate on economic development and the well-being of our people. And Asean countries have demonstrated that they know how to do this. Now together with our new members the Southeast Asian countries can cooperate and help each other to prosper economically. That way we will become internally stable and less susceptible to the kind of outside pressures our detractors like to apply.

Economic prosperity is really the answer to our security problems because with prosperity Asean will be taken seriously and its views respected. It is for this reason that whenever our Foreign Ministers meet it is usual for the major economies of the world to have Ministerial dialogues with us. Even on matters of security we have devised a regional forum in order to trash out perceived problems. No other regional organisation has such an arrangement. Military strength may inspire fear but it will lead to a costly arms race. The benefits will only accrue to the manufacturers and traders in the weapons of war. Economic prosperity inspire respect but at a much lower cost, while the benefits remain with us.

In December of this year, the Heads of Government of all the Asean countries will meet informally here in Kuala Lumpur. It will be an epoch-making gathering for the Heads of Government of nine countries of Southeast Asia will be meeting as leaders of one of the world's strongest regional groupings. There will be a lot of serious things to discuss, decisions and stands to be made. They will not be just celebrating 30 years of Asean but also have serious regional and international matters to discuss.

The world now talks glibly of a borderless world, of the Information Age, of open markets and open societies. Asean, a group of developing countries will need to know how all these new concepts about international commerce and politics will affect us. It is wonderful to know that all the huge markets of the developed countries will be open to us in exchange for our opening up of our tiny markets. But can we really gain access to these markets. Or will the removal of border cause a flow in one direction only.

Presently we see a well-planned effort to undermine the economies of all the Asean countries by destabilising their currencies. Our economic fundamentals are good yet anyone with a few billion dollars can destroy all the progress that we have made. We are told we must open up, that trade and commerce must be totally free. Free for whom? For rogue speculators. For anarchists wanting to destroy weak countries in their crusade for open societies, to force us to submit to the dictatorship of international manipulators. We want to embrace borderlessness but we still need to protect ourselves from self-serving rogues and international brigandage.

Already we are seeing giant companies swallowing up chunks of the business in the developing world. They monopolise the services sector through their huge shipping, airlines, insurance companies and banks. The media, print and electronic are now controlled by them throughout the world. We are denied press freedom by the many people who trumpet press freedom. Only bad news about us are published, the good news are often buried in their archives.

We worry, we should worry about this borderless world of the Information Age and the free market. We are not rejecting it out of hand. But we should know where we stand. We should know how we are going to handle the problems which will arise. Already they have formed powerful regional trade blocs. And eight of the most powerful nations have decided that they, and they alone, should determine the fate of every country. When they agree on anything, as for example the revaluation of the yen, we have to pay the price. And when they quarrel we will be trampled under.

Alone, none of the Southeast Asian countries will be able to protect itself. But nine Asean countries with half a billion people may be able to do something to help ourselves.

We are glad that when the leaders of the Asean nine meet, there will also be a meeting with the leaders of the three biggest economies in Northeast Asia. We will then have an opportunity to present our views on a whole lot of international issues to them, for their economies are closely linked to ours. What affects us will affect them too. We abhor trade blocs but we do need as many countries to understand our problems as we can find. We may be moving towards a borderless world, but we also see greater exclusivity on the part of the rich. More than ever we need to win friends, even from among the exclusive group.

In this region we believe in a prosper-thy-neighbour policy. This is not due to altruism. It is really motivated by selfishness. Prosperous neighbours make good trading partners and give each other less problems. The problems of poor neighbours tend to spill over their borders. It is for this selfish reason that we reject beggar-thy-neighbour policies.

But we must not be passive in the exercise of this prosper-thy-neighbour policy. We should actively help each other. Certainly the newer members of our Association are going to need help in order to catch up with the older members. I believe there is an Asean formula for success, for how else can we explain why every Asean country has shown rapid economic growth and political stability? We must help every country to make use of this formula so that we can all be stable and prosperous.

Once again I would like to stress the importance of being economically prosperous. Prosperity is essential for the avoidance of internal conflict. Former American Secretary of State Robert S. McNamara noted that the incidence of (internal) conflict had been highest in the poorest countries and lowest in the richest. In helping our fellow members to prosper, we are in fact helping to reduce conflict in our countries. With this we will all prosper and be conflict-free. And we as neighbours will benefit from the wealth and the absence of conflict in our region. Again we see the selfishness in the policy to prosper your neighbours.

There are roughly half a billion people in the Asean member countries now. They are not the richest people but even though per-capita income may be low, their total purchasing power is still considerable. Besides, with their high growth rates their economic clout must increase rapidly. Their low cost of production, the skills and the diligence of their people are assets which will make them attractive to investors and traders alike. The future is indeed bright for the countries of the Asean. We know what we must do collectively. We know what we must do individually. And we have the strength to do what is best for us and to defend ourselves. If we fail, we can blame no one but ourselves. We must not fail. That must be our resolve.

I would like to bid welcome to all the distinguished delegates to the 30th Asean Ministerial Meeting and to all our honoured guests. This meeting makes a milestone in the history of Southeast Asia. It is also a milestone in the history of regional cooperation. We believe in strength through unity. We reject exclusivity. We suffered in a bipolar world. We know now that a unipolar world is no better. We know that alone we each will suffer. Only through being together can we maintain and benefit from our hard-won independence.

24

Asean and East Asian Countries Should Enhance Cooperation

"With the onset of globalisation and the resultant borderlessness of countries, the need to collaborate and foster strategic alliances, either bilaterally or multilaterally, becomes urgent. Only by working together can a robust and sustainable growth of this region be achieved."

THE Asean-East Asian Business Forum and the Asean SMIs Showcase 1997 launched three days ago are efforts jointly organised by Malaysia with support of the Asean Secretariat and the Japanese government through JETRO. Such efforts are indeed commendable as they lend substance to the close

---

A speech delivered at the Asean East Asian Business Forum in Kuala Lumpur, Malaysia, on August 7, 1997

relationship of Asean countries together with Japan, South Korea and China. This positive cooperation and business linkages are the only way to ensure the prosperity and sustainability of this region.

The Asean and the East Asian economies as a region is huge in terms of land area, population, resources, markets as well as the potential for growth. At present the levels of development differ from country to country. Priorities and the abilities to transform our economies into competitive global players also differ, each pursuing its priorities and pace of development in the best possible way they know. However, combined together, the region can be a formidable force especially with the huge economic potential of this region.

With the onset of globalisation and the resultant borderlessness of countries, the need to collaborate and foster strategic alliances, either bilaterally or multilaterally, becomes urgent. Only by working together can a robust and sustainable growth of this region be achieved.

Asean economic cooperation appears to have contributed towards its successes but by comparison to the E.U. it is minimal. What has happened is that Asean countries are quick to learn from each other about economic development. This success has been more through individual effort, although a peaceful environment and frequent consultations have contributed. Nevertheless, they have been almost uniformly successful with Singapore, Malaysia, Thailand and Indonesia ranking among the leading top 22 trading nations. Asean has also been an attractive region for the flow of cross investments both from outside and within the Asean region.

Asean's new members, Laos and Myanmar, and perhaps the entrance of Cambodia at a later stage, would offer potential investors with an integrated region of economic opportunities. By then, there should be a more cohesive Asean collaboration in the areas of transport, energy and communications, infrastructure development, science and technology, agriculture as well as environmental preservation. With the new Asean image and a population of almost 500 million people, the region is poised to be a strong market for investors and businesses in the near future.

The economic dynamism of the East-Asian region continues to make great stride, the result of sustainable growth in exports especially manufactured goods and increase in the flows of foreign direct investment (FDI). The East Asian countries in particular, Japan, South Korea and China have made significant contributions to world trade.

Set against this scenario, it is envisaged that in a decade, Asean will emerge as a unified Southeast Asia sharing common goals and economic vision, anchored on a desire to see the region becoming a boon to investors and businesses alike. This scenario implies that adjustments need to be made in the way investors and firms operate in the region. Under the new trade and industrial environment, companies are expected to locate themselves not to just serve one particular Asean country market only, but to look at Asean as one large market.

It is expected that under this circumstance, a major challenge to Asean will be to keep international trade open. As open trading system has been a key factor that supports the development of the Asean region, it is in Asean's interest to ensure that this open global trading environment continues to provide a supportive and conducive framework to enable the region to sustain and further enhance liberalisation efforts.

In the context of dynamic economic growth, the role of small and medium-sized industries (SMIs) will be considerable. Worldwide, SMIs constitute more than 80 per cent of the economy. This sector therefore assumes an important role in the economic development of both developed and developing economies. In most countries, SMIs have been the source of employment, augmenting rural income, stimulating indigenous innovation, creativity and indigenous technologies. With changes taking place globally in terms of competition, ways of doing business and changes in the trading and investment environment, SMIs must be prepared to undertake changes in order to survive competition and to be an important contributor to economic development.

In the midst of this wave of change, the agility and ability to adjust and respond flexibly to the market needs and demands are essential to SMIs. While the government can provide some assistance and facilities to spearhead the development of SMIs, it is for the entrepreneurs themselves to use their creativity and innovative strategies to build up their market niches, both domestically and globally. Towards this end, the competitiveness of SMIs can no longer be relied on cost efficiency alone, for equally important is the ability to offer products, or services with higher quality and greater value added, at internationally competitive prices.

The SMIs must not only concentrate on building up entrepreneurial expertise, but be competitive in the ever dynamic marketplace. They must be vigilant and be able to keep abreast of the changes in the international trading environment and be able to produce and export world-class products in order to remain competitive. In meeting these challenges, SMIs in this region must adopt a global perspective of manufacturing and marketing operations, investing in the right type of technology and processes that can contribute to efficient production, undertake R&D to develop new and improved products, as well as embark on the promotion and marketing of products and services to gain significant market shares.

Unlike some East Asian countries such as Japan and South Korea, SMIs in most Asean countries are still weak in terms of inter-firm linkages with their larger counterparts. These linkages are important to ensure the strengthening of the industrialisation base of the economy in addition to providing market access as well as the opportunities for cross border transfer of technology and sharing of technical expertise. It is therefore the task of organisations in the respective Asean countries to learn from these East Asian countries and to try to adopt and adapt the strategies to suit the requirement of each country.

As the new millennium sets in, SMIs must assume a greater and more important role in enhancing and strengthening the economy of Asean and the East Asian countries. The demands of market liberalisation measures, of global trade and economics provide challenges and opportunities for SMIs. Indeed, the different levels of economic development of Asean and East Asian countries provide opportunities for developing and forging common strategies to exploit the complementarities in resource endowment and capabilities.

The Asean-SMIs Showcase '97 and the Asean-East Asian Business Forum therefore provide an avenue for those involved in the manufacturing industries, directly or indirectly, to meet, discuss and share their experiences with each other in developing SMIs in their respective countries. Most of all it is envisaged through the business matching sessions, participants of this forum will bring home meaningful and rewarding results.

The initial contact established should be further nurtured into concrete businesses and joint ventures. Indeed, with the staging of these events, industrial linkages between Asean and the East Asian countries will be further enhanced, especially with the realisation that the Asean and East Asian countries will indeed be the key to strengthening the global economic interlinkages in the next decade, turning the area into one of the most competitive marketplaces in the world.

25

Greater Economic Integration in Asean

"In moving towards greater economic integration, Asean may need to look at the way we cooperate with a new perspective. Our targets must be that of gaining advantage from our strengths rather than merely protecting our weaknesses. We had struggled hard to gain independence and we cannot afford to lose our sovereignty in the name of free, unrestricted breaching of our economic and other borders."

I RECALL addressing the 1st Asean Economic Congress ten years ago here in Kuala Lumpur and posing the challenge then for Asean to establish a closer, more constructive and complementary relationship in the area of economic cooperation. Today, we are proud that our collective

---

A speech delivered at the 29th Asean Economic Ministers Meeting in Petaling Jaya, Malaysia, on October 16, 1997

resolve has brought us the first harvest of tangible results. Ten years ago, the idea of a free trade area in Asean was not acceptable. It was seen as a move that would slowly erode national sovereignty. Today we are into the fifth year of the implementation of the Asean Free Trade Area (AFTA) an initiative that has achieved much greater success than the previous Preferential Trading Arrangement (PTA). Intra-Asean trade last year amounted to US$155.2 billion, a ten-fold increase over that in 1987 when it amounted to US$14.7 billion. Over 95 per cent of that trade is covered by tariff concessions under the Common Effective Preferential Tariff (CEPT) which will lead towards the realisation of AFTA.

When we embarked on AFTA, we were not addressing it solely to increase intraregional trade within the Association. The larger markets for our goods lie outside Asean and that the prospect for expansion and realising regional growth lies with the international market. We need AFTA to increase competition and upgrade the efficiency of our industries in order that they become more competitive in the world market. This would in turn make Asean an attractive area for long-term non-speculative FDI and attract more world class producers to locate their operations in the region. I would like to remind ourselves that the bigger the intra-Asean trade, the more attractive will we be to the serious FDI.

Our thrust forward require us to go beyond tariff reduction. Asean's own involvement in industrial production needs to be nurtured along with FDI to deepen and to share in the benefits of growth. We in Asean agreed to upgrade industrial cooperation by introducing the Asean Industrial Cooperation Scheme (AICS). We also realised that the services sector will be the key sector to develop greater competitiveness and widen the base of economic growth of Asean. To achieve this, we concluded the Framework Agreement on Cooperation in Services and launched negotiations in market access beyond our commitments to the General Agreement on Trade in Services (GATS). We reviewed action plans in the sectors of transport and communications, energy and minerals while at the same time we provided greater focus in our plans for cooperation in the food industry, agriculture, forestry, and tourism. We also concluded a Framework Agreement on Cooperation in Intellectual Property to ensure that our region will provide effective protection for intellectual property, both foreign and domestic. Protection for the former will further raise the confidence of foreign investors while protection for the latter is essential as our own entrepreneurs now have the capability and capacity to produce works, systems and inventions. We are also formulating guiding principles towards the formation of an Asean Investment Area (AIA) which foresee a freer flow of capital as well as effect transparency and predictability of policies and practices in investment, with a view to making the Asean region a haven for investors.

Given the mutually reinforcing initiatives put in place by AEM, I have no doubts that as we move into the first five years of the next millennium, Asean economic cooperation would be brought to the "higher plane" that was envisaged by the 4th Asean Summit in Singapore in 1992. However, to remain on this higher plane, we need to set our sights higher. To make Asean relevant in the next millennium we need to have a longer-term vision of what we want to be as an Association. Twenty five years from today do we foresee Asean becoming a common market like the former EEC? Are we setting our sights to be a single market or an economic union a la the E.U.? What is certain is that we need to make the bold move towards greater economic integration, as we will have to face an uncertain environment. Our recent experience with currency manipulation should be a big lesson for us. While we should always avoid abusing the system, we must be perpetually alert to the possibilities of others exploiting our weaknesses in order to weaken us further. We have a duty to bring order within and between our countries, and indeed contribute to a more orderly world environment.

What is clear to us now is that the challenges which we will have to face will be enormous.

First, while we are closer to achieving the vision of our founding fathers for Asean to embrace all ten countries of Southeast Asia with the membership of Laos and the union of Myanmar and the eventual membership of Cambodia, we need to remind ourselves that the development gap between the old and new members require special attention.

We need to step up the pace of our collective development efforts in order to stay ahead of change. We have to encourage the new members to face change with greater determination if we are to benefit from such changes. I see the Mekong Basin development initiative serving as the primary vehicle for us to collectively spur economic development of the new members. Through this initiative, we can work together in developing much needed hard infrastructure such as roads, bridges, railways, airports and ports, industrial estates, schools, hospitals and the like as well as soft infrastructure such as education and training, trade and investment facilitation, improvements in administration and management of projects. This regional effort will not only benefit the riparian states, but also the region as a whole. Our resolve to assist the development of the riparian states must be matched by deeds and financial commitments on mutually beneficial terms.

Second, we need to liberalise without ignoring the dangers posed by those who see only the opportunities afforded them by their strength and experience and the weaknesses which their victims may have. We must not just think of level playing fields but also the relative strength of the contestants. While standing together to face problems may not amount to much, but it is much safer than isolating ourselves in the hope that we may not be noticed and thus left alone.

Some postulate that the future of the world will be characterised by herd behaviour and herd instincts. The different herds will wheel to the left or the right or will charge ahead, trampling upon whatever may be in the way. This does not speak well of the progress human civilisation has made. But then, the history of human civilisation is full of the exploitation of the weak by the strong and the powerful.

Third, we need to ensure that the multilateral trading system remains fair and open. We were able to contribute positively to the conclusion of the Uruguay Round by exerting a positive influence on the debate on issues and by our actions in effecting orderly liberalisation measures. We have continued to exert Asean's influence during the WTO Ministerial Conference last December to ensure that extraneous issues and non-trade issues are not brought within WTO disciplines. It is important that the WTO becomes the sole organisation for the settlement of disputes. Actions taken outside the WTO should not be allowed and should not be respected. An organisation must have rules in order to exist and be relevant. Such rules must have the force of law, international laws which are properly and democratically enacted. An organisation without rules and regulation will not result in equality of benefits for the members. Liberalisation is not about doing away with rules and laws altogether. It is about everyone submitting to the same set of rules, regulations and laws on a world scale rather than national scale.

Fourth, we have to embrace the positive aspects of the development of capital markets. Developments in our capital markets over the last five months revealed how vulnerable we are to various abuses. We must make a distinction between speculative short term hot money operations and serious investments in productive activities. We should continue to welcome real long-term investments but must be wary of operations which do not create any real wealth for us. We need to cooperate in macroeconomic policy formulation to ensure the achievement of stable, sustainable economic growth for the region.

Fifth, we need to harness benefits from developments in Information Technology very early before the enormity and speed of these developments render it impossible for us to catch up. The conduct of trade and commerce itself has not been spared from the development of IT. Electronic Commerce is the buzz word that we need to embrace. Early discussions have begun on the need to formulate a framework for electronic commerce. Whether we are conscious of it or not, all of us in Asean have conducted part of our business transactions using modalities that form part of electronic commerce. We need to engage ourselves in the discussions to formulate a framework for electronic commerce to ensure that the guiding principles within that framework do not put us at a disadvantage but in fact places us all in a position to reap maximum benefits. We cannot ignore that we need revenue in order to govern ourselves and much of this revenue comes from commercial activities.

Sixth, we need to upgrade, strengthen and expand our services sector to complement our strength in the manufacturing and industrial sector. The latter cannot remain as the only engine of growth as its contribution to GDP has almost reached the optimum while the lack of strength in the former has been highlighted as a major contributor to the current account deficit in most of Asean economies.

Seventh, we must continue efforts at upgrading the knowledge and skills of our people with greater vigour if we are to keep pace and move ahead of change. We must also continue to emphasise raising productivity levels in all activities.

In moving towards greater economic integration, Asean may need to look at the way we cooperate with a new perspective. Our targets must be that of gaining advantage from our strengths rather than merely protecting our weaknesses. We had struggled hard to gain independence and we cannot afford to lose our sovereignty in the name of free, unrestricted breaching of our economic and other borders. At least we must ascertain that such breachings will be subjected to eventually beneficial rules.

We have also to acknowledge that as we move towards greater economic integration, we are more exposed to the occurrence of disputes among ourselves in the implementation of the economic initiatives that we may put in place. We have to resolve such disputes swiftly and effectively. The Agreement on Dispute Settlement in Economic Initiatives concluded in April this year provides the much needed reference.

While we implement initiatives towards greater economic integration in Asean, we must not overlook the critical element of reducing transaction costs or the cost of doing business in Asean. We need to review regulatory and administrative procedures at the national and Asean levels with a view to making them more simple and transparent and ensure that new measures introduced have the effect of facilitating decisions and approvals. We have to combat corrupt practices squarely.

Towards reducing the cost of doing business we will have to review the efficiency of our utilities industry. The cost of electricity, gas, water and telecommunications will be less of a burden to business if we liberalise the more restrictive regulation. In the same vein, we need to make our ports and airports more efficient, our haulage and freight forwarding services more responsive.

At the same time, we have to adopt processes that are sustainable, clean and environment-friendly to avoid costs associated with environmental degradation. We have to educate and encourage our rural population to do away with antiquated practices in their daily economic activities which can pollute the environment. The proximity of our borders requires that we address the problem of pollution from both the national and regional perspectives. Failure to do so will most certainly cost us a lot and will retard our progress.

Asean economic cooperation has come a long way from the time when we embarked on our first collective economic initiative 20 years ago. The journey ahead is longer and more demanding. We can make the journey less onerous if we prepare ourselves well for it, if we remain focused in addressing issues that confront us and if we remain committed to achieve our regional goals.

26

A Private Sector Salute to Asean

> "And our private sector must work closely with our public sector, in each country and in the region as the Asean entity. We had achieved so much in the past through our cooperation, through our constant consultation and through our strong support for each other. Now more than ever we need to continue that cooperation, consultation and support."

THE Association of Southeast Asian Nations (Asean) has undergone tremendous changes and development for the past three decades. Our achievements are the result of hard work of both the government and private sectors. Without the latter economic development of the region would not have

---

A speech delivered at the Conference Commemorating Asean's 30th Anniversary in Petaling Jaya, Malaysia, on December 13, 1997

been as high as it is. Therefore, it is appropriate that today we gather for a meeting called "A Private Sector Salute to Asean". Let us utilise this conference to take stock of our achievements and setbacks as well as plan for greater success in the years to come. Let me acknowledge at the outset, that the success which we hope to achieve will only materialise if we—the government and private sector—continue to work closely together in harmony and single-mindedly for the betterment of the region.

Asean has come a long way since its founding in 1967. We started off with just five countries—Malaysia, Singapore, Thailand, Indonesia and the Philippines. In 1967, no one gave us much of a chance to succeed. Southeast Asia had by then undertaken two short-lived attempts at regional cooperation, first in 1959 with the formation of the Association of Southeast Asia (ASA) and then in 1966, Maphilindo, which grouped Malaysia, the Philippines and Indonesia. Politically, Southeast Asia was divided according to whose colony we once were. Thailand was of course never colonised. The Indochinese countries were either at war or faced various insurrections after decolonisation. Differences in ideology kept us apart and at times resulted in confrontations. There was a great deal of suspicion of each other made worse by conflicting territorial claims. We tended to align ourselves with one or the other of the two blocs in the bipolar world and their Cold War strategies. The outlook then was indeed bleak.

Today, the situation is very different. In thirty years, Asean has evolved into the pivotal organisation in the Asia-Pacific region and is also the most successful regional organisation in the developing world. Although there still exist certain differences, challenges and conflicting claims, the region nonetheless enjoys unprecedented peace and stability as well as tremendous economic development. With a market of almost 500 million consumers, Asean is often considered as the gateway to the broader East Asian market. Although all of us are facing economic turmoil which has undermined our growth, our potential is still there. It is reasonable to expect us to recover and to forge ahead. We still have a not unreasonable hope to catch up with the developed West. The skills and the willingness are still there. The system and the game rule of a globalised world may not favour us now but we will learn to handle them in time and we will bounce back, possibly stronger than before. What we need to do now is to build up our internal strength, our organisation and our unity and then we will overcome.

Today we have almost made a reality of the aspiration of Asean's founding fathers by admitting Laos and Myanmar. We had hoped that Cambodia would have joined us by now and so complete the Asean dream. But that is not to be yet. We hope that it would not be too long before the whole of Southeast Asia belong to one group.

Many question the wisdom of our admitting countries which are so different in terms of ideology and economic system. I would like to point out that in 1967 when Asean was formed, the differences between the five founding members were more marked. Indeed, they were almost at each others' throats. Suspicions between them were deeper. There were serious unsettled conflicts between them.

But they came together anyway and persisted in their attempts to find common grounds for cooperation. There is no reason to assume that the differences that the new Asean members present to the grouping cannot be handled by people who had already exhibited their skill at compromise and diplomacy. They will succeed, and they will succeed more quickly if they are left alone and their efforts are not subverted by outsiders.

The members of Asean have shown a distinct tendency to be flexible. They are not dogmatic and they are ever ready to learn and adopt strategies which had brought success to other members. It is no accident that all the Asean countries appear to progress uniformly towards economic success. It is reasonable therefore to expect the new members to do the same and build a regional grouping of developing countries which will be second to none.

Today the Asean countries, in particular the more successful members are faced with economic turmoil. It would be wrong to say that their governments and their people, in particular their businessmen are completely blameless. There had been many abuses and malpractices, including of course large foreign borrowings and deficits in the balance of payment. These abuses on their own would have resulted in slowing down growth or even reversing it. But the devaluation of their currencies had precipitated matters, magnified the scale of their economic reversals, and caused financial turmoil. It had exposed and bankrupted not only the bad companies but it had rendered good companies non-viable. It had put banks and other financial institutions in danger and forced their closure. Indeed, it had forced countries to borrow heavily from international agencies and obviously increase their debt burden.

It will be very many years before the economies of Southeast Asia regain some semblance of their past performance. Some say it will be a matter of months. Can it be so quick when we see that despite the loans they have taken, despite the stringent and prudent actions they have been forced to take, despite the dismissals and unemployment, the economy is not only not recovering but it is actually sliding further backwards? It is flattering to be told that we will recover quickly but proud independent countries would not surrender their economic and political freedom if recovery could be so easily managed. In any case can recovery be real if there is no sovereignty?

We in Southeast Asia should accept that we are poor now and the road to recovery is going to be long and hazardous. If we are going to make it, if we are going to shorten the time, we need to stay closely together. We have a need to develop an Asean-wide strategy for recovery. It is not going to be easy especially as we are no longer free agents. But there is still much that we can do together.

In the first place the good understanding and cooperation that the Asean private sector had developed with the governments of Asean countries must be continued and enhanced. Whatever we may have to do to overcome our problems we will have to do together. We will of course not go against our undertakings to whatever international agencies we have committed ourselves to. But those undertakings will not paralyse us completely.

Since all our currencies have been devalued to almost the same extent, the exchange rates between us have not changed much. We can therefore continue our trade with each other almost as we did before. Indeed, we can expand our trade greatly, if our regional sources retain this competitiveness. It is up to us to do so.

AFTA can be reexamined in order to expedite and expand it. If AFTA is considered good during times of prosperity, cannot it be good or even better during times of stress? Much will depend on our ingenuity and our Asean spirit of unity and belief in mutual help. I feel quite sure that the devaluation of our currencies can facilitate trade between us. There are many things which we could not buy from each other before which should be competitive now if we keep our new exchange rates and the price of goods according to the domestic markets. We have discovered in Malaysia that palm oil, for example, is priced in U.S. dollars even for the local market and yet our costs are in devalued ringgit. While we do not grudge the windfall profit our exporters get due to the devaluation of the ringgit, we think that the domestic market should not be burdened by the extra profit which palm oil producers would get by selling in the domestic market at export prices.

I realise of course that palm oil is not something that we buy from each other. But supposing we adopt an AFTA pricing system it would be cheaper than edible oil imported from outside AFTA. And there are many products with the same marketing mechanism as palm oil.

Many economists assume that devaluation of a currency automatically result in increased competitiveness and windfall profits. This is not necessarily so. A lot of the exports of Southeast Asian countries have contents imported from countries with currencies which have appreciated against us, the U.S., for example. The imported contents reduce the cost advantage from devaluation. Freight and insurance also do the same, both inbound and outbound. A 40-per-cent depreciation would not give a 40-per-cent advantage.

If the product with imported contents is sold locally there will be a price increase. This increases the cost of living. There will be demands for wage increases which will increase local cost further. In the end the benefit from devaluation will be totally lost.

If we want to make AFTA worthwhile we have to guard against the inflationary effect of devaluation. It is not impossible to do this. It requires a great deal of discipline among our people. But the result of the increase in trade between the countries of Asean will help cushion off the effects of devaluation and shorten our recovery period.

When Malaysia promoted a buy-Malaysia campaign we were accused of economic nationalism. It is not nationalism at all. When our currency is devalued effectively it makes imported goods dearer by the same percentage of the devaluation. To continue buying we will have to find more ringgits to convert to the currency we have to pay for the imported goods. The ringgit has depreciated by 45 per cent. How do we find 45 per cent more ringgit to pay for the imports? Indeed, in our present economic condition we cannot even find the amount of ringgit we used to use to pay for the imported goods. We actually have less ringgit now because business is bad and wealth is not being generated. So how can we buy the old amount of imported goods? What we can buy is much less than the percentage of depreciation of our currency. We are not being economically nationalistic. We are just unable to find the money to buy. You cannot impoverish us and then tell us to continue buying what you sell.

What is true of Malaysia is also true of all the other Asean countries who have suffered devaluation. But since relative to each other's currency the devaluation has not been so high, it follows that goods from Asean countries would be cheaper for Asean countries. Of course we would prefer to sell outside of Asean in hard currency and earn more foreign exchange. But where we can be competitive in each other's market we should buy Asean.

I am not advocating Asean economic regionalism. But the fact is that we have less money now and we should buy from the cheapest source. There should be no restriction to others entering our markets with their products but if their prices are higher we should not buy from them. As a last resort we could barter in order to increase our trade since we don't know when the pressure on our currencies will be lifted.

What I am suggesting does not negate market forces. Market forces demand that we buy the cheapest and the best. By taking advantage of the simultaneous devaluation of our currencies, the Asean countries can actually increase their trade with each other without keeping out other countries. That way we will help each other's economy to recover and hopefully to grow. When we are rich again and able to afford the imported goods and luxuries from outside Asean, we should do so. Indeed, we will be helping to restore world trade by working hard to recover quickly.

I would like to suggest that the private sector in all the Asean countries seriously examine this idea. Perhaps governments too should examine it. We may reject it as a harebrained idea in the end but there is no harm in examining every possibility of restoring the health of our economy. We must always be prudent and correct but in business and in finance there have always been new ways of making money. We have lost our wealth largely because we have not understood what is going on in the big wide world outside. For 30 years we had developed our countries the old-fashioned way. We believed in hard work, in sweat, toil and tears. We believed that one good turn deserves another. We believe in cooperation between countries, within regions and between regions.

But during the 30 years concepts and ways of doing business have changed. With liberalisation, globalisation and market forces came herd instincts. We were caught unawares. And so we have to pay a price, a heavy price. But for the price that we paid we should at least get a few tips on how to manage if not a full lesson.

We know we have to accept what we cannot reject. We are doing our best now. What is not viable must be killed outright so the survivors can be free to consolidate their positions. People unnecessarily employed should be retired.

As a doctor who once practised surgery I appreciate the need to amputate gangrenous legs to save the rest of the body. What we have to do is surgical. And we will do it. We must reassure the world that we will carry out what we have undertaken to do, at whatever cost. We hope that in the end we will restore confidence and the wealth will flow back.

In the meantime, we must nurse our association, Asean. On this 30th Anniversary we must renew our pledges and our commitment towards building a region of Peace, Freedom and, hopefully, Prosperity. We must stand together linking arms and bolstering each other's strength.

And our private sector must work closely with our public sector, in each country and in the region as the Asean entity. We had achieved so much in the past through our cooperation, through our constant consultation and through our strong support for each other. Now more than ever we need to continue that cooperation, consultation and support. What had stood us in good stead in good times must now be made to stand in good stead in bad times. Some have accused us of the denial syndrome. The denial would be greater if we don't admit that we are facing a serious problem which can return us to our colonial past. The journey back will not take months as our admiring detractors smilingly assure us. It is going to take years and years of hard work and new cunning. But God willing, we will return, battered, bruised but we will return.

The private sector has many reasons to salute Asean. Having saluted let us now put our heads together and work out the return to our past achievements.

27

Asean's Response to Financial Crisis

"Asean's responses to the challenges confronting the region have created the impression of an Asean in disarray, its members at odds with one another. Malaysia believes that the maintenance of positive interstate relations, has to be consciously nurtured."

IT has been one year since the 2nd Asean Informal Summit in Kuala Lumpur, when we discussed as a group the financial problems that afflicted our respective economies. By all counts, the last year or so has been the most difficult and challenging period for all of our countries. Despite our

---

A speech delivered at the 6th Asean Summit in Hanoi, Vietnam, on December 12, 1998

best efforts to prevent a deepening of the problem, the financial turmoil nonetheless developed into an economic crisis.

After a decade of impressive growth, most of us in the region are now confronted with zero or negative growth for 1998. In Malaysia, we expect our GDP to decline by 6 per cent or more this year. At the worst point of the crisis, the Malaysian ringgit was devalued by the currency traders by some 60 per cent against the U.S. dollar while our stock market lost two-thirds of its capitalisation, i.e., more than US$200 billion. As a nation and a people, we have become impoverished. Our banks and corporations almost collapsed.

In responding to the crisis, Asean countries have instituted various macroeconomic measures and financial reforms. Although Malaysia is not a recipient of International Monetary Fund (IMF) assistance, our initial approach was to implement a virtual IMF approach. We discovered that these measures worsened the economic situation. And they failed to restore foreign investor confidence. As the international community refused to do anything, Malaysia had no choice but to change direction on its own.

When the financial crisis began Malaysia called for regulating the activities of currency traders to prevent our economies from rapid impoverishment due to devaluation by currency trading and attacks on the stock market. While capital inflow can promote economic growth and improve the wealth of our peoples, sudden and massive outflow can destroy whole economies. The existing international financial system is not equipped to deal with massive capital flight and the resultant financial and economic turmoil.

The powers that be preferred instead to blame the governments of the affected countries for all kinds of misdemeanours. Instead of reining in the currency manipulators they allowed them to destroy the economic tigers in order to force them to seek help and accept IMF prescribed reforms.

Malaysia cannot afford to wait while the developed economies and international financial institutions dawdle. We have therefore instituted our own National Economic Recovery Plan (NERP). We removed our ringgit out of reach of the currency speculators. We also ensured that shortselling of our shares and the consequent fall in value was stopped. Relieved of the threat of devaluation and destruction of our companies and banks we were able to implement measures to revitalise our economy.

Through lowering interest rates, increasing liquidity, recapitalisation of banks and managing the NPL as well as many other measures we have succeeded in arresting the decline and set the economy back on the road to recovery. What we have done is merely to insulate ourselves from the predatory speculators. Otherwise, our economy is as open as before. Foreign investment can and are coming in, trade goes on undisturbed and profits can be repatriated. The Kuala Lumpur Stock Exchange (KLSE) remains open to foreign investors subject only to the retention of investments in stocks for one year. Capitalisation of the share market has doubled since the measures were implemented.

I would like to point out that currency and the share market were controlled before. We liberalised because we believed in the free market. But our liberalism was abused, resulting in economic and financial depression. We have no choice but to reimpose controls. Until the international community agrees on an international regime that will remove the kind of dangers we have been exposed to, we will have to continue with our controls.

The recovery of our respective economies in Asean can be expedited only in an improved regional and international environment. Thirty years of Asean cooperation has given Southeast Asia the stability and solidarity which contributed to unprecedented economic growth and rising standard of living. Unfortunately, the economic crisis severely tested the resilience of Asean member countries. Our Association, and relations between its members, have come under some strain.

Asean's responses to the challenges confronting the region have created the impression of an Asean in disarray, its members at odds with one another. Malaysia believes that the maintenance of positive interstate relations, has to be consciously nurtured. Asean has the wherewithal to pull through this turbulent period. I am referring here to the Asean approach, its method of work, and the principles governing the conduct of relations between member states. These are contained in various Asean declarations, treaties and statements evolved through the years. We should adhere to them.

This Summit Meeting should help create an environment conducive to positive relations and regional growth. I am therefore pleased that the Hanoi Declaration which we will sign later and the Hanoi Plan of Action which we are going to adopt, have reiterated the many principles and undertakings upon which we commit ourselves.

Malaysia strongly supports initiatives aimed at strengthening regional economic cooperation and consolidating the economic fundamentals of Asean member countries. We will cooperate with our Asean partners to strengthen and to insulate the region from external disturbances as much as possible. We continue to support greater economic integration and the acceleration of the Asean Free Trade Area (AFTA).

The economic crisis has impoverished Asean economies and undermined national stability. Millions of people have been thrown out of work while others have their purchasing power drastically reduced. Businesses, large and small, have been bankrupted. The social well-being of the people has been disrupted. Malaysia thus welcomes the proposed measures contained in the Hanoi Plan of Action to promote social development and address the immediate social impact of the financial crisis.

Malaysia particularly looks forward to the 2nd Asean+3 Summit involving the leaders of China, Japan and South Korea. Because of their economic weight, the policies and measures of these three East Asian countries have significant impact not only on regional but also on the global economy. Malaysia appreciates the commitment of China not to devalue its currency, its efforts at economic reforms and domestic growth. Malaysia welcomes the reform being undertaken by Japan of its financial sector and the Japanese initiative in providing a package of support measures totalling US$30 billion to help Asian countries overcome the current economic difficulties.

The financial turmoil has underscored the many challenges inherent in globalisation. Even as we embrace it, we must be wary of the dangers which accompany it.

Malaysia welcomes the decision of the G7 Finance Ministers in October to strengthen the international financial system. But we must remember that they are looking at it from their exalted position. Our problems may not receive their attention. We have to find a more suitable forum to discuss our needs.

28

Asean's Vision 2020: Moving Forward

"In Asean's Vision 2020, the leaders of Asean and the countries of Asean resolved to create a stable, prosperous and highly competitive Asean Economic Region in which there is a free flow of goods, services and investments, a freer flow of capital, equitable economic development and reduced poverty and socioeconomic disparities."

ASEAN is now one generation old. On December 15, 1997, at the 2nd Asean Informal Summit held in Kuala Lumpur, the Heads of Government of Asean adopted Asean's Vision 2020. I agree fully with that Vision 2020.

A speech delivered at the Asean Business Summit 2000 in Kuala Lumpur, Malaysia, on April 11, 2000

Now is the time not of words. Now is the time for action. The need of the hour is not for new formulation and concepts. The need is for the transforming of our brilliant vision into palpable reality.

Our vision, already agreed to by all of us in Asean is of a concert and a community of Southeast Asian nations, outward looking, living in peace, stability and prosperity, bonded together in partnership in dynamic development and in a community of caring societies.

These words are not mine. They belong to all the leaders of Asean, to all the peoples of Asean.

Under Asean's Vision 2020, we envision the Asean region to be, in 2020, in full reality, a Zone of Peace, Freedom and Neutrality, as envisaged in the laration of 1971.

By the year 2020, Asean should have established a peaceful and stable Southeast Asia where each nation is at peace with itself and where the causes for conflict have been eliminated, through abiding respect for justice and the rule of law and through the strengthening of national and regional resilience.

We envision a Southeast Asia where territorial and other disputes are resolved by peaceful means.

We envision the Treaty of Amity and Cooperation in Southeast Asia functioning fully as a binding code of conduct for our governments and peoples, to which other states with interests in the region adhere.

We envision a Southeast Asia free from nuclear weapons, with all the Nuclear Weapon States committed to the purposes of the Southeast Asia Nuclear Weapons-Free Zone Treaty through their adherence to its Protocol. We also envision our region free from all other weapons of mass destruction enabling us to develop and prosper.

In December 1997, the leaders of Asean resolved to chart a new direction towards the year 2020 called, "Asean 2020: Partnership in Dynamic Development" which will forge closer economic integration within Asean.

We reiterated our resolve to enhance Asean economic cooperation through economic development strategies, which are in line with the aspiration of our respective peoples, which put emphasis on sustainable and equitable growth, development strategies which enhance national as well as regional resilience.

We pledged to sustain Asean's high economic performance by building upon the foundation of our existing cooperation efforts, consolidating our achievements, expanding our collective efforts and enhancing mutual assistance.

We committed ourselves to moving towards closer cohesion and economic integration, narrowing the gap in the level of development among member countries, ensuring that the multilateral trading system remains fair and open.

In Asean's Vision 2020, the leaders of Asean and the countries of Asean resolved to create a stable, prosperous and highly competitive Asean Economic Region in which there is a free flow of goods, services and investments, a freer flow of capital, equitable economic development and reduced poverty and socioeconomic disparities.

We resolved, among other things, to maintain regional macroeconomic and financial stability by promoting closer consultations in macroeconomic and financial policies.

We resolved to advance economic integration and cooperation by fully implementing the Asean Free

Trade Area and accelerating liberalisation of trade in services; by realising the Asean Investment Area (AIA) by 2010 and the free flow of investments by 2020; by intensifying and expanding subregional cooperation in existing and new subregional growth areas; by further consolidating and expanding extra-Asean regional linkages for mutual benefit; by cooperating to strengthen the multilateral trading system, and by reinforcing the role of the business sector as the engine of growth. We resolved to promote a modern and competitive small and medium enterprises (SMEs) sector in Asean which will contribute to the industrial development and efficiency of the region.

We pledged to accelerate the free flow of professional and other services in the region, to promote financial sector liberalisation and closer cooperation in money and capital market, tax, insurance and customs matters as well as closer consultations in macroeconomic and financial policies.

The leaders of Asean, in their wisdom or should one say with their common sense, committed themselves to enhancing human resource development in all sectors of the economy through quality education, upgrading of skills and capabilities and training.

The countries of Asean committed themselves to world standards and a conformance system that will provide a harmonised approach to the free flow of Asean trade, while meeting health, safety and environmental needs.

We see vibrant and open Asean societies consistent with their respective national identities, where all people enjoy equitable access to opportunities for total human development regardless of gender, race, religion, language, or social and cultural background.

We envision a socially cohesive and caring Asean where not only hunger, malnutrition, deprivation and poverty are no longer the principal problems but also an Asean community where strong families as the basic units of society tend to their members—particularly the children, youth, women and elderly; and where society is empowered and responsible and gives special attention to the disadvantaged, disabled and the marginalised, where social justice and the rule of law truly reigns.

In Kuala Lumpur in December 1997, we also resolved to develop and strengthen Asean's institutions and mechanisms to enable Asean to realise the vision and to respond to the challenges of the coming century. We also saw the need for a strengthened Asean Secretariat with an enhanced role to support the realisation of our vision.

Asean realises all these. Thus following on the Kuala Lumpur Asean Vision 2020, we saw the Hanoi Plan of Action, a realistic set of action plans.

At the risk of boring you with repetition, let me repeat the need, now, for action, real, palpable result-oriented action.

The principal business of Asean is not exclusively business. It is the making of peace and friendship and concerted collective action by us all in this region of Southeast Asia.

But you will see that we in Asean understand fully the central importance of the business sector. We know who lays the golden egg. And we are not going to kill the goose. Rather we are going to nurture it, to care for it because we appreciate its role.

What I have tried to outline to you is Asean's way forward in the short, medium and long term.

Let me now make some remarks on three key issues that we all must focus upon. These key issues are indeed the keys to our achieving our goals. These issues in simple one-word terms are: (i) globalisation; (ii) liberalisation; and (iii) mega-mergers.

There is a lot that is good about globalisation. It provides us many opportunities. We are not selfish. We do not mind others getting the opportunities also. But we must ensure that the opportunities and the benefits accrue to us as substantially as they do to others.

We had thought of globalisation in terms of FDI, of inflows of capital, technology and market access. But our recent traumatic experience has shown that globalisation can also mean massive outflows of capital in order to impoverish and weaken us and to prepare us for foreign takeovers of our businesses, and possibly our countries too.

The question is can we have the good the globalisation can bring and reject the possible destruction and subjugation of our economies?

Many of us will reject the alarming prediction that we will be colonised again. We are independent countries and we will remain independent. But if we have to submit to the dictates of others, dictates, which are not only demeaning but also deleterious to our interests, can just having our own governments be sufficient to prove that we are not being colonised?

But the fact is that globalisation can be good, very good for us. It can be good if we have a say in its interpretation. It will be good if we can have some control over the movements across our borders, across all borders in fact movements not just of financial capital but also of other forms of capital.

Admittedly the countries of Asean will see things differently. We will disagree among ourselves. But if we disagree too much we will become divided in our approach towards globalisation.

May I then call upon all of us to say this about globalisation before we say 'yes' to it. We should say:

> No globalisation without benefit,
> No globalisation without self determination,
> and
> No globalisation without corporate
> responsibility or conscience.

The first 'no'—No globalisation without benefit—is the rationality imperative.

The second 'no'—No globalisation without self-determination—is the freedom and independence imperative. We did not fight to be free of the old imperialism in order to have the privilege of bowing before the new imperialism.

The third imperative is about ethics, morality and responsibility. We rightly expect everyone—politicians, children, grandmothers, padi planters, fishermen, and union leaders to have ethics, morality and responsibility. Why must some of the followers of market theology say that as for business and corporations, inserting the sacred mantras into their wallets and holding it in their breast pocket, close to their hearts, is all that is necessary?

I have mentioned the rationality imperative. I have mentioned the freedom and independence imperative. The ethics, morality and responsibility imperative demands the third 'no': No globalisation without corporate responsibility and conscience.

I am afraid I cannot accept the unconscionable. If this upsets anyone, I am sorry. I make no apologies. As a human being, I believe no human being can accept the doctrine that business can do whatever they like, governments should allow business to do whatever they like, and if bones are crushed and lives are ruined, it's all right.

It's too bad. It is simply the market. It is that wonderful abstraction, 'the market', the god that can do no wrong, that can be expected to perform better and to produce better results than anything that individual human beings either in business or public life can do.

Since I became Prime Minister of Malaysia, my country has seen the fastest rate of marketisation of its economy in its history. We did it not out of ideological commitment or theological faith. We did it because it yielded results.

The market still has a great deal to deliver. We must continue to marketise the Malaysian domestic economy. But those who believe in market miracles and divine perfection need not a heart transplant as much as a head transplant.

On the issue of liberalisation, let me also say that we must distinguish between domestic liberalisation and cross-border liberalisation, between national market liberalisation and international market liberalisation.

For my country, my government and I remain committed too much greater national market liberalisation. This must, of course, be subservient to the rationality imperative, the freedom and independence imperative and the ethics, morality and responsibility imperative.

We cannot have a headlong rush to national market liberalisation, oblivious of the need to ensure the proper regulatory and transparency framework, the issues of sequencing, and readiness.

We cannot rush headlong, simply because 'the good book' and bible-totting 'world' 'experts' from Washington tell us that it is good for us. I apologise to those who say 'Go for the so-called big bang' even if it blows up in your face. I apologise to the eager beavers who say: 'Proceed to the cutting edge' even if you are cut to bits. I apologise to those experts who say: 'Just hold the good book, close your eyes and jump', even if it is in the dark of night and the hole is bottomless. Don't worry. Just keep the faith.

I also believe that in Malaysia, as in all countries, we cannot afford to rush headlong without considering the issues of equity and distribution, balance and fairness.

At this stage of the game in Malaysia and on the global battlefield, I have far, far fewer reservations about national market liberalisation than about international trade and financial liberalisation.

Without doubt, there is a lot that is good in both international trade and financial liberalisation. The good should be imbibed and the opportunities should be exploited. But again let me stress the imperatives of rationality, of freedom and independence, and of ethics, morality and responsibility.

Even as we say a qualified 'yes' to international liberalisation, we must say:

> No international liberalisation without benefit,
> No international liberalisation without self-determination,
> No international liberalisation without regulation,

> No international liberalisation without representation, and
> No international liberalisation without corporate responsibility and conscience.

With regard to the first, it is absolutely clear that for most countries in this world, the benefits of international liberalisation are blindingly unclear, while the costs of international liberalisation have so far clearly outweighed the benefits. We in Malaysia should not forget that while massive FDI did come to Malaysia in 1999, last year only 1.2 per cent of global FDI was destined for the whole of the African continent. We received several times more than all the 30 countries of Africa put together.

Perhaps it is too early in the game for calculating the costs and benefits to the developing world to become clear. If it is too early, why the rush to negotiate a whole series of new international trade liberalisations? More lack of consideration or something worse?

With regard to the second 'no'—no international liberalisation without self determination—let us not forget what one of the great leaders of Asean, Ho Chi Minh, said a long time ago: nothing is more precious than freedom and independence.

With regard to no liberalisation without regulation, who wants a brave new world without rules, where businesses are free to do as they please, where, like agent 007, they have a licence to kill? Why do they want such a brave new world beyond their borders when they would never consider unfettered, unregulated markets and complete anarchy at home?

As for no liberalisation without representation, I seem to recall one of the rallying calls of the great

American fight for freedom from colonial tyranny: no taxation without representation. If the physical life and death of our people, not merely their welfare, are at stake, why is there such a strong fight to prevent democracy, to ensure against democratic representation? Why are we not to be allowed to have a say? Can we, should we, accept a world where the rules by which we must live or die shall be unilaterally determined?

My views about businesses, which feast on and cause untold human misery have been stated. I shall not repeat. But let me end with what must be our third worry or should we call it a 'nightmare'?

Every day, we see the news on the global mega-mergers.

The global media laud it as if it is the next best thing to motherhood and apple pie. These global mega-mergers are good for equity investors, in the grips of 'irrational exuberance', eager on 'a feeding frenzy'. Both these terms are not mine.

These global mega-mergers may be great for others. But the question has to be asked: is it good for us? The biggest conglomerates in Asean are as ants in comparison with these elephants. Is it not interesting that despite the fact that every market guru and every market theologian can easily refer to the evils of oligopoly and monopoly in the free-market bible, the free-market priesthood is silent or even enthusiastic? Why is this so?

I have raised many issues in this speech. It is quite obvious that all of us in Asean, in the developing world and in the developed world have a lot of independent thinking to do. Repeating all the sacred text from the sacred books brought out to us by experts who have the look of the incredibly committed Christian missionaries of the 19th century simply will not do at the dawn of this, the 21st century.

I believe that today, as ever in the past, as it must be in the days to come, it is essential for us to think independently and to act, driven by the dictates of rationality, the imperative of freedom and independence, and the demands of ethics, morality and responsibility.

29

Asean: An Economic and Political Force Today

"So far ideas about the shape of things to come have originated from the rich West. It is time that the poorer nations of the world, Asean countries for example come up with ideas, which can shape a more equitable world."

I AM greatly honoured to have been selected to receive the Asean Millennium Award. The conferring of such an award is also an added honour to Malaysia. On behalf of my country, allow me to express my deepest appreciation to the Asean Business Forum, in particular to its Board of Directors, for choosing me for this award. Malaysia is as much aware of the honour as it is aware of the responsibilities

---

A speech delivered at the Asean Achievement Millennium Award in Singapore on September 10, 2001

given the current pressing challenges confronting Asean. The consensus around the Asean Business Forum reflects confidence in Asean but equally it also reflects legitimate expectations on the part of other members of Asean.

I am grateful for this opportunity to share with you some thoughts about Asean, to think aloud, as it were, about this Association of ten nations in the Southeast Asian region. Looking back on the history of Asean, its creation was premised upon the need for a forum to discuss largely the problems of managing relations between newly independent nations whose historical backgrounds were rather different and who were almost forcibly kept apart. The early leaders of the Asean countries were strangers to each other, as were the people. Indeed, they were suspicious of each other, aggravated by territorial claims and differences in their political perceptions.

Under such conditions the initial contacts were mainly social of the getting-to-know-you kind. It was only gradually that barriers were broken, first between the leaders and then between the people. In time however it became a habit for Asean leaders to meet wherever international conferences take place. Then business leaders and other groups got into the act. Precedents and traditions were established as for example the custom of new leaders of Asean countries visiting the other leaders upon their assumption of office.

The differences are still there but they have not hindered cooperation on economic matters and even on certain aspects of international politics. Much remains to be done but there is little doubt that Asean is a very real grouping that has benefited the members in their dealings with each other and the rest of the world.

Today, Asean has become an economic and political force that has to be reckoned with in the region. Since its inception 34 years ago, it has already achieved a degree of cohesion, unity and capacity for concerted action that has elicited quite respect and emulation by many other regional organisations of developing countries.

This is partly due, I believe, to the nature of Asean's inception in which rare statesmanship played a role and laid the ground for Asean's spirit of solidarity and its sense of common purpose in the face of pressures and challenges coming largely from outside as the prosperity of Asean countries attracted the greedy and the unscrupulous together with the serious investors. Common interests also lead to cooperative action for economic and social development, adherence to the principle of peaceful settlement of disputes, and scrupulous observation of the principle of non-interference in the internal affairs of member states. These attributes provide the bases for Asean's rapid development, its attitudes, policies and the conduct of its relations with other countries.

In essence, the nations of Asean, both collectively and individually, have made significant contributions to the peace and stability of the region by their political pragmatism and economic dynamism. While pursuing their national priorities, Asean governments never fail to take into account the larger interest of the region. For Malaysia the conduct of its policies and relations with its Asean neighbours fitted well with a policy premised on the belief that prosperous neighbours will not only have less domestic problems which impact on neighbours but, can actually help prosper it by being a richer trading partner. It therefore pays for neighbours to help prosper each other.

Asean as a group can obviously contribute much towards the growth and advancement of the region. Asean's Vision 2020 provides an outward and forward looking Asean, living in peace, stability and prosperity, bonded together in partnership for dynamic development and in a community of caring societies. To achieve this vision, one must not forget that economic development is the most important factor that will contribute to growth and stability. That is why in Asean, we would like to see more economic integration put in place, and it is for this reason that we have conceived the idea of the Asean Free Trade Area (AFTA).

As can be seen, Asean is moving towards a truly integrated economy. Trade barriers are coming down. Tariffs on almost all products traded by Asean nations will be down to 5 per cent or zero in just a few short years. Even now products of companies with related operations in two or more Asean countries may flow freely within the region with tariffs of at most 5 per cent or none at all.

Trade among Asean countries is being made easier with the harmonisation of standards and procedures. Infrastructure linkages including transport, energy and telecommunications are being expanded and strengthened. Together we are projecting the Asean region as a very attractive place to invest and to do business.

In this regard, under the Asean Investment Area (AIA), which was adopted by Asean, foreign investors could take advantage of privileges offered under the AIA. Asean countries are also opening up and giving national treatment to other Asean investors including joint ventures between Asean and foreign companies.

There is also the Asean Industrial Cooperation Scheme (AICS), which gives AFTA treatment to products traded within Asean by companies operating in two or more Asean countries.

Given the rapid expansion of electronic commerce in the global economy and recognising that our future competitiveness depends on our ability to develop and use information technology, Asean is now focussing on the application of information and communication technology to enhance trade. Asean is now developing an action plan on the necessary infrastructure to promote e-Asean.

I personally wish to reemphasise the importance of the physical linkages between Asean countries so as to further facilitate Asean economic integration. At the Asean Informal Summit in Singapore last year, Malaysia proposed the Singapore-Kunming Rail Link (SKRL) project, which our own experience in railways shows that it can be a powerful catalyst for economic development. There were also proposals for the Asean highway network, the Asean Power Grid and the Asean Gas Grid. All these present enormous opportunities for investment and would stimulate other forms of investment and economic activities.

In looking forward towards the free flow of products and services in Asean, we must not forget the financial crisis that hit our region four years ago. The precipitators of the crisis were the unscrupulous rogue currency traders. They saw nothing other than profits for themselves. The serious social, economic and political turmoil they created in their trail is of no concern to them. The financial crisis of 1997 halted the spectacular growth of Asean's economy. FDI inflow fell from US$28.1 billion in 1997 to US$16.1 billion in 1999. The per-capita income of Asean which stood at US$1,384 in 1997 was reduced to US$930 in 1998, a drop of 33 per cent. Many people were left without jobs as companies could no longer bear the rising costs of doing business. Those people who were laid off had to feed their families and matters were made worse when the IMF insisted that subsidies for food, cooking oil and fuel must be stopped. The result was predictable. The people turned violent and this only contributed towards even greater deterioration of the economy, to making recovery even more difficult. Still the blame is on the governments, on their corruption and lack of transparency, etc. That these same governments were the ones which had so miraculously developed their countries and made them economic tigers was forgotten or ignored. The rogue currency traders and the international financial system, the IMF and the World Bank were regarded as blameless.

The Asian financial crisis is not over yet. It will not be over until the international financial system is changed and those who abused it are curbed. For a time there was talk of a new international financial architecture. There were a few meetings of selected nations but the whole thing has fizzled out. It looks like nothing is going to change.

But now globalisation is being promoted aggressively. We have had a foretaste of globalisation when the currency traders devalued our currencies and precipitated a financial crisis of unprecedented severity. Are we going to accept globalisation without question, a globalisation conceived and interpreted by the rich countries, which is manifestly in their interest?

Nowhere should the Asean countries be more united than in the negotiations for a new world economic order as will happen at the WTO. The first round of the negotiation had resulted in various undertakings by the proponents, which to date have not been fulfilled. We have not seen the flow of capital in the direction of developing countries, which we are told would happen. Indeed, we have seen just the opposite, a massive outflow of capital from our countries, which has almost completely destroyed our economies. Now a new round is proposed in which non-trade issues, such as labour standards, human rights, democracy, child labour are to be linked and made conditions for trade and investments.

These issues are important and they should be promoted but there are other forums for discussing them and making them conditions for trade and investments will retard the growth of many developing countries. The rich countries had taken more than a century to reach their present status of social, economic and political sophistication. It is unrealistic to expect developing countries to achieve such levels of sophistication overnight. Linking these issues with trade and investments will surely impose tremendous strains on poor developing countries. Instead of their sharing in the wealth they are likely to become poorer and poorer, while the rich wax ever richer.

But what is frightening is the preparation being made by the rich to take full advantage of the WTO and the free borderless market. We see the huge corporations and banks of the rich already merging and acquiring each other so that they become colossal and unbeatable. Only a few players will be left in every major field. Banks, manufacturing industries, transport corporations, etc., are now being consolidated through mergers and acquisitions so that the small and the weak would just not be able to compete and survive.

Perhaps, this will be good for efficiency, although I doubt it. But when business corporations become richer and bigger than most nation states, they will want to dictate to the whole world so as to cater to their unlimited greed. Nations will cease to be independent. They will become just units for the servicing of the great banks and corporations.

You may notice that at a time when the world is insisting on the rule of law by governments, there is a demand that governments should deregulate trade and business. It does seem that governments must be curbed while big business should be allowed to do what it likes. The market is supposed to regulate itself, which is nonsense of course because the market is not in the business of promoting good social and political behaviour but in making as much profit as it can for the players.

Clearly the trend in globalisation is towards maximising the opportunities for the already rich to make more and more money at the expense of the sovereignty of countries and the social, political and economic needs of the countries.

Some Asean countries may believe that they can deal and even benefit from the present interpretation of globalisation. And well they may. But it behoves us to look closely at the proposals and the agenda of the WTO. We must know fully and exactly what are the possibilities and dangers which the new international economic regime will pose for us before we agree to a new round of WTO talks. We want to know exactly how have the rich countries complied with the agreements reached during the first round.

If Asean is to be meaningful it must look after the interest of all its members.

Asean countries must come together to negotiate the demand for a new round of WTO talks. There must first be consensus among Asean countries on the need to review the agreements reached at the first WTO.

Following that a new agenda must be drawn up which must exclude extraneous matters. The effect on all countries, rich and poor must be fully understood and assessed before any support can be given to the formulation of a new international trade and investment regime.

Since countries are at different stages of development it is unrealistic to insist that everyone must adopt standard policies and practices. The poor must be given a lot of leeway, protection and time. The rich are not going to be destroyed if there is some delay and some regulations in the implementation of standard practices. We have already seen how one medicine to cure all financial ills have precipitated serious widespread and intractable crisis in the Asian countries. We do not want to see a continuous crisis for the whole world arising from an ill-considered world trade regime.

Asean is credible and relatively strong. It can play a role to bring about a more equitable world economic order. It must not think of its own interest only. Certainly it must not allow the interest of an individual country to supersede that of the group and the region.

The world is still very primitive. In terms of might is right our civilisation has not progressed beyond the stone age. Who can kill more people determines who can have his way. It is unconscionable that today more than three-quarters of the world are poor while a small number of people are as rich as whole countries. Wealth must be more equitably distributed.

The world is extremely rich in resources, human and material. There is no reason why any country should be poor. It is entirely possible for wealth to be more fairly distributed. At present the globalised world with its huge free market is benefiting only a select few people, rich people with the capital to take advantage of the borderless world.

It is common for the people who acquire wealth in a country to give some back to the nations through taxes on incomes and profits. By the same token people who wax rich because the globalised borderless world afforded them unlimited opportunities for profits should return some of their profits to the world. The money can be used to build needed infrastructure in the poor countries, infrastructure which as we all know will stimulate economic development. When the poor are enriched, they will be more ready to buy the goods and services of the rich.

Clearly the rich will not lose by paying for the infrastructural development of the poor. They will get back their money many times over. So the rich should accept that as the rich citizens of a borderless world they should pay a minute tax to be used to help the poor.

So far ideas about the shape of things to come have originated from the rich West. It is time that the poorer nations of the world, Asean countries for example come up with ideas, which can shape a more equitable world. Taxing the rich international businesses can be one such idea. I hope Asean countries will dare to advocate this idea.

I thank you for the honour conferred on me and for giving me this opportunity to give the views of a universal recalcitrant.

30

Asean: Surviving in the New Economy

"So how do we survive in the new economy? We survive by staying together, by defending our market and by extracting the best terms from our dealings with the developed countries. Alone we will fall, but together we stand a chance. Each of us will be offered attractive propositions but we will lose out if we break rank."

THIRTY YEARS is a mere blink of the eye in the history, but for Asean it is a lifetime. Still Asean's achievements in this short period can be matched by few regional organisations. To understand Asean, it is important for us to look back and reflect on Asean's past struggles, triumphs and tribulations. For more than a century, the countries of Southeast Asia

---

A speech delivered at the 7th ASCOPE Conference and Exhibition in Kuala Lumpur, Malaysia, on November 7, 2001

were colonised and subservient. They were not their own masters and they could do nothing for themselves. Theirs was to produce the raw materials cheaply for the industries of their colonial masters thousands of miles away. But at last they gained their independence. Unable to cope with this newfound freedom they confronted each other. But very quickly wise counsel prevailed and the leaders founded Asean as an organisation of neighbours wishing to live in peace with each other. Asean was not an economic grouping at first but inevitably it became one. Today Asean ignores the political differences between them in the greater interest of economic development through cooperation.

We are not yet a union as the European countries are but we have achieved a degree of cohesion seldom experienced by other regional organisation. If not for the currency crisis of 1997-98, we could have become an association of economic tigers.

We competed with each other of course but we also cooperated and we learnt much from each other's failures and success. We became a force in the formulation of the relations between nations, the trade and exchange of the world, the setting of standards and practices for a better international community. We were able to present the views of the developing countries effectively and so protect their interests.

It is Asean that gives impetus to the regional infrastructure linkages that support and attract investments. The road that Asean countries have travelled spans areas involving energy, trade, security, education, training, formulation of best practices and energy infrastructure.

Cooperation in trade and regional security has been the cornerstone of Asean's success. As we forge ahead into a more uncertain world, the intrinsic value of such solidarity will be of paramount importance, in order to enable us to deal with other countries and regions from a position of strength. More importantly, such solidarity has resulted in the provision of effective social and economic safety nets in which Asean as an entity can depend on.

In keeping with developments in the ICT front, we are also positioning the region to be e-ready. The e-Asean platform will be the vehicle for Asean countries to promote and facilitate ICT development in the region. A two-prong approach is adopted, firstly, investments in ICT will be the new engine for driving economic growth and secondly increasing ICT infrastructure will provide the means for Asean people to progress through better education, knowledge and skills.

A great deal of our success has been due to trade and regional cooperation. Greater consensus and a policy of non-interference in the internal affairs of member countries has enabled the region to survive the severe test of strained relationships. Instead of interfering in the domestic politics of member countries, we propound the principle of "prosper thy neighbour" to ensure that all the member countries are helped to achieve prosperity through the right kind of economic policy and management.

Among the steps taken to build up the economic cooperation of the member state is the agreement to form an Asean Free Trade Area. Industrialisation of a country depends much on the size and purchasing power of the domestic market. On the other hand, economies of scale contribute much to the viability of an industry, especially the big capital-intensive industries. By combining the markets of the countries of Southeast Asia, a good size market can be created.

Industrialisation of the region can then be more feasible. However, there must be some understanding on the distribution of the industries. If all the countries want the same industries then there will be only small national markets for each, not regional markets. The economic community would then fail.

Another problem is the hijacking of the market by foreign interest. Seeing the potential of the much enlarged markets, foreign corporations would bid to monopolise it by setting up so-called "national industries" which are owned by them, while the locals will only work for them with little ownership and technology transfer. The products would be cheaper and the quality world class but the small local companies would be locked out and indigenous industrial capacities will not be enhanced.

We would be no better off than when we were the raw material producing colonies. The only difference is that we are now the low-cost assemblers of foreign products. Of course, we need and we want FDI, but they must be for increasing our exports to other regions and where possible they should give a fair share in the industry to the locals if they are after the lucrative Asean regional markets.

Globalisation is being pushed aggressively and we should accept that globalisation is the future of this world. However, we need to modify the interpretation of globalisation. Presently globalisation is only about free capital flows in and out of countries, about market opening and abolition of discrimination in favour of national companies. In preparation for globalisation the giant banks and industries of the rich are merging and acquiring each other in order to become huge and unbeatable. The tiny local banks and industries would stand no chance of competing with these giants. Once the borders are down these super big foreign giants would move in to take over the local financial and industrial sectors of the small countries.

Maybe it is good for business and even good for the consumers. But it will not be for long. National interests such as the well-being of local people, their level of skills, their participation and independence in business and occupation will not only be neglected but may even be restricted. Even governments may lose the power to determine policies and to exercise their powers. They will have to cater to the demands and even take instructions from the powerful foreign banks and companies, which control the economy completely.

The Asean countries have already experienced one manifestation of globalisation, namely the manipulation of their currencies by international currency traders backed by such institutions as the IMF and the World Bank. Suddenly the East Asian economic tigers became impoverished as their money was devalued through shortselling. Not only were they forced to borrow from the IMF but they had to submit the management of their countries' finances and economy to the IMF.

Whether by design or not the advice given by the IMF resulted in worsening the economies of these countries. Their businesses began to fail. They were then forced to allow in foreign corporations and financial manipulators who bought the near-bankrupt banks and businesses at fire-sale prices.

Despite the obvious failures of the international financial regime and the Bretton Woods institutions like the IMF and the World Bank, no attempt is made to restructure the system. Currencies of developing countries are still exposed to devaluation by the currency traders. Businesses and investments have still to face the uncertainties of fluctuating currency exchange rates and bear the costs of hedging.

Globalisation may be inevitable but there is no reason why globalisation should be solely for the purpose of free flows of capital. The rate of globalisation can be staggered so that the developing countries need not give up completely the protection of their industries yet should be able to access the market of the rich so as to grow their own economies. This is not as unfair as it sounds. *Quid pro quo* and perfect reciprocity should be between equals. When the players are of unequal strength or capacity, handicap should be allowed the weak in order to compensate for their weakness.

Today we see the rich countries taking unilateral action in order to protect their industries. Not only do they impose countervailing duties when there is suspicion of dumping but they now restrict imports simply because their own industries are hurt by cheap imports. This is a retrogressive step as far as globalisation is concerned but the rich are apparently privileged to disregard even agreed convention. If the rich can do this to protect themselves surely the poor should be given the right to protect their puny businesses.

In a globalised world should there be only giant banks and giant industries and businesses? We are fast moving into an impersonal society. Big organisations may be efficient and cost-effective, although I don't think this is necessarily so, but big organisations cannot have personal relations. In the e-world, relations between people are already impersonal enough. If added to this we have to deal with people at the fringes who cannot possibly have a full commitment to the business being done, we are going to lose all the friendship and personal attention of business people we deal with in our daily life.

Small businesses have not really stifled our growth. If they had we would not be where we are today. Little one-branch banks, Mama-and-Papa provision shops and restaurants, even backyard industries have contributed towards our economic growth. We could interact with them personally, bring our problems to them and know that they value your customs.

We should have our big, efficient businesses of course but we must ensure that the small ones survive also. If we have to protect them then we should. The globalised world should not be so uniform that no matter where we are in the world, our hotels, restaurants, TV programmes, newspapers and magazines, motor vehicles, banks, indeed everything would be exactly the same. Variety is the spice of life. The spice is fast disappearing as we stay in Hilton Hotels, eat McDonald's hamburger, drive in a Ford car, bank with Citibank and buy our household needs from Carrefour. Already we cannot tell where we are once we enter the lobby of our hotel. They all look the same.

Brands have become so important that new makes especially from developing countries find difficulty in entering an established market. The Italians monopolise the brand names so much so that Asians have to invent Italian-sounding names for their products. A developing country can never hope to market its own vernacular brand. And so we are uncompetitive even before we start. Since we must allow foreign brands to enter our markets, our unprotected brand cannot make headway even in our own country.

Asean countries must learn to be competitive of course. But it is not so easy to play the game of catching up with established people from the developed world. We cannot even depend on producing and exporting raw materials because the terms of trade are not going to favour us. Manufactured imports will always be appreciating in price much faster than the price of our raw materials.

So how do we survive in the new economy? We survive by staying together, by defending our market and by extracting the best terms from our dealings with the developed countries. Alone we will fall, but together we stand a chance. Each of us will be offered attractive propositions but we will lose out if we break rank.

Asean has a market of half a billion people. No doubt their purchasing power is low but we can build that up by helping each other to develop. With this market we can leverage a trade off so that access would be on our terms, on terms that will give us some substantial advantage.

The Asean market and the development of our economic wealth must be done by ourselves. Trade between Asean countries is big but it can be much bigger. We must use our closeness to advantage by maximising the sourcing of our needs from within Asean where possible. We must build up our industries based on the larger Asean market rather than on national markets. We have to agree on a distribution of industries by siting certain industries in specific countries so that competition would be minimal though not to the extent of a monopoly.

The Asean electrical and gas grid must be made a reality as quickly as possible. The railway and road networks should also be linked. Travel between Asean countries should be facilitated by using a common smart card for travelling or border crossing.

The various growth triangles must be seriously developed so as to take advantage of each other's particular strength, i.e., manpower, natural resources, capital and technology.

There are clearly a host of things that the Asean countries can do in order to survive in the new economy. Certainly in the field of energy as have been pointed out, the power and gas grid linking the Asean countries can help us to benefit from easy access to power. And power, cheap power, is essential to make us competitive. To survive in the new economy we have to seek and develop every competitive advantage that each one and together we have.

31

China: A Challenge Or an Opportunity for Asean?

"The emergence of China as an economic powerhouse should not worry Southeast Asian countries any more than in the past. There will be challenges and there will be opportunities. Faced with these the Southeast Asian countries will have to learn to manage the challenges and seize the opportunities."

IN 1803, almost exactly 200 years ago, Napoleon Bonaparte gave us a most prophetic quotable quote. "China is like a sleeping giant," he said. "And when she awakes, she will astonish the world." Astonish the world China truly has. Of this there can be no doubt.

A speech delivered at the 8th Nikkei Conference on the Future of Asia in Tokyo, Japan, on May 21, 2002

But many questions remain. The organisers of this 8th Nikkei Conference on the Future of Asia have asked me to speak on this astonishing China, this phenomena of the awakening giant and what it portents for us in the Asean countries. Is it going to be what someone describes as a black hole which sucks up everything and gives back nothing or will China be the locomotive for the economic prosperity of Asean in the future?

What one has to accept is that China is there. It has been there for the past 4,000 years and it cannot be wished away. The idea of containing it, a policy tried by the West in the Cold War years did not work. If China was a non-performer during those years it was not because of containment by the West but because the Chinese leaders chose to isolate China and to reject modernisation.

Now China has decided to join the rest of the world in espousing trade and development and like it or not we have to admit that China is doing well and blossoming into a great economic power. A country of 1.3 billion diligent and skillful people, organised and disciplined cannot but be a powerful country once it sets its mind on developing its huge potential. As an economic power it will exert much influence in the affairs of the world. China must therefore be accorded its rightful place in the constellation of powerful nations.

The fear is that with its enormous power it may try to expand into Southeast Asia, perhaps territorially. China's occupation of Tibet may be cited. But China has no history of expanding territorially. It may have had pretensions about being the centre of the world, the Middle Kingdom, but historically China had not colonised other countries. In contrast the European countries conquered and colonised Asian countries thousands of miles away from Europe. I don't think

China is about to change its ways and become a colonial power.

The clash involving China in the future is going to be economic and it will be between China and the other developed countries. Now we all know that when two elephants fight the grass and the animals underneath will get trampled. So the fear is not from China's black hole character but the fierceness of China's struggle for market share for its products and services worldwide.

For Asean what will be the effect of China's economic struggle? Well, we have already seen how China's attractiveness as an investment location has reduced the flow of FDI to the Asean nations. China's advantage at the moment is its low-cost labour and the enormous size of its domestic market.

But we have to remember that Japan too started as a low labour-cost country. It did not remain so for long. As Japan prospered the cost of labour rose quite rapidly. Such was the increase that Japan had to invest and produce in low-labour cost countries of Southeast Asia very early on in order to remain competitive. Additionally the voluntary and involuntary transfers of technology resulted in Southeast Asian countries developing their own industrial capacities. Thus Japan's industrialisation benefited the poorer Asean countries in a number of ways.

It is possible that China too will progress in the same way. Already the labour cost along the coastal areas which have developed first is higher than that inland. As industrialisation proceeds the cost in China is bound to go up. The size of China's population will make this process longer than in Japan. Still there will be some benefits to be derived as China's workforce begin to earn higher incomes. We are already seeing this in Southeast Asia as attested by an increasing influx of Chinese tourists. We are also beginning to see Chinese investments and increases in their imports of certain products including electronic goods and components.

When 1.3 billion people get even a slight increase in income the purchasing power will be enhanced much more than happens in an ordinary-sized country. China's growing prosperity cannot but make it a great market for Southeast Asia. Trade with China has already increased manifold since the opening up of the country. The momentum is gaining and we can expect faster growth, especially after China's accession to the World Trade Organisation (WTO).

But perhaps I am being too optimistic. China is an economic threat for Southeast Asia. It is already a threat in terms of attracting FDI and it is going to be a threat to Southeast Asia's world trade. We know that China with its cheap and highly skilled labour and the potential of its huge domestic market is capable of large-scale, low-cost production of anything and everything. It has been gradually putting in place the legal and policy frameworks and infrastructures for FDI and domestic investments and its products are going to be highly competitive. Just as the Japanese and the Korean products displaced European and American products, we can expect Chinese products to shoulder aside not only the Japanese and the Korean but also the products of Southeast Asia. Chinese goods will achieve world standards and already we are seeing signs of Chinese innovation resulting from their own Research and Development.

In the household appliances business this is already happening. Japan, South Korea and Southeast Asia will lose their market share for these low-tech yet essential goods. Of course the Europeans and the

Americans are not ever going to be able to stage a come back. And it is likely that China will dominate the market for other manufactured goods as well. However, there will be niches where branded goods of high quality produced by some countries will continue to be in demand.

Besides, China cannot so impoverish other countries especially Southeast Asian countries so that they cannot buy Chinese products. It is imperative that China ensures the survival and prosperity of the countries which will be its market. And this may mean increasing Chinese investments in these countries and increasing purchases of raw materials and components produced by these countries.

We can infer that this will happen from the Western response to the influx of cheap high quality Japanese goods. They focussed on developing brands of quality and prestige. Thus the numerous brands of European goods, motor vehicles, watches and audio equipment. As niche products the market is not big but the profit margins are enormous. The European strategy is still working and I believe Japan, South Korea and Southeast Asia will be opting for niche products of high quality and prestige.

Japanese mass produced products are not inferior but because of snob value, European products do find a market. Similarly, when the markets of the world are flooded with Chinese products, a good number of buyers will be opting for branded goods from traditional suppliers. Southeast Asian products can provide the demand for variety and name. Obviously so can Japan and South Korea.

The race is already on and Southeast Asian countries are already looking for niche products and businesses involving hi-tech and I.T. Some Southeast

Asian countries do have certain advantages, including geographical location, good legal and educational system, values and practices with which the international business community is comfortable.

The governments of these Southeast Asian countries are more business friendly and workers do not often resort to industrial action. The political stability and generally calm atmosphere are good selling points. Besides the local entrepreneurs and local capital have become sophisticated and knowledgeable about investments and manufacturing as well as being familiar with the world market.

It is well to remember that together the Asean ten have nearly half the population of China. Their average per capita is as high as China, and the domestic markets obviously have the same potential as China. Given a period of peace and stability the Asean countries can grow and develop and become an attractive market and continue to be a good location for FDI.

Asean is one of the most cohesive of regional groupings involving developing countries. With the Asean Free Trade Area (AFTA) the Asean countries have become more attractive to foreign investors wishing to operate in the bigger Asean market. Already motorcar manufacturers are investing in Asean countries in order to take advantage of the larger market as well as taking advantage of the relatively lower cost and highly skilled labour. It is very likely that manufacturers of other products would follow. A well developed infrastructure and good supporting industries make investing in Asean countries a sound proposition.

Trade between the Asean countries is increasing rapidly. The AFTA will act as a stimulus to more intra-Asean trade. Obviously Asean will not be a walk over for China. Life would be tougher. FDI will diminish. The export led growth will not be easy any longer. But the Southeast Asians will be able to find a niche for themselves. Working together they will be able to use their combined market to match that of China.

A symbiotic relation can be developed between China and Southeast Asia. A rich China will need quite a lot of things that China cannot produce by itself. And China's needs for everything would be enormous. Malaysian and Indonesian palm oil should find a ready market in China. So would pulp and paper, oil and gas and chemicals which the availability of feedstock gives a competitive advantage to quite a few of the countries of Southeast Asia.

So far I have talked largely about the economic challenge posed by China. Although China has never attempted to conquer and colonise as Europeans were wont to do, the fact remains that there are huge Chinese minorities in all the Southeast Asian countries. In fact, in Singapore, the Chinese majority is such that Singapore today is basically a Chinese state with Malay and Indian minorities. This Chinese minority invariably dominate the economy of the Southeast Asian countries.

The situation is such that the Chinese can become a fifth column in Southeast Asia. In fact, in the immediate post Pacific War period the Chinese resistance movements against Japanese occupation converted itself into revolutionary forces bent on establishing Chinese communist states in the countries of Southeast Asia. When China came under communist rule a lot of sympathy and support was extended to the Chinese guerrilla forces which at first fought against the colonialist British and later the independent governments of Southeast Asian countries.

The insurrections were by and large unsuccessful.

Today the people of Chinese origin in Southeast Asian countries are loyal citizens. Admittedly, a few still would like to make these countries into extensions of China by demanding that the Chinese as Chinese be separated from the indigenous people, by having a Chinese education system, separate and segregated Chinese schools and the preservation of all that is Chinese. But these people, few in number, do not get the support of the majority of the Chinese who wish to live in peace with the indigenous people and to do business and acquire wealth.

We do not believe that the Chinese in Southeast Asia have any wish to contribute towards China's overseas territorial ambitions or adventures. In fact, we think that they are not only loyal citizens but they are good bridges for the economic cooperation between China and Southeast Asia.

Today the relationship between China and Southeast Asian countries is good. There is, of course, the dispute over the islands in the South China Sea fuelled by the possibility of finding gas and oil there. But serious confrontation has been avoided.

The policy with regard to defence differs between the Southeast Asian countries. Some would like to have the American military shield but some would like to see a less confrontational stance. Malaysia believes that if we treat China like a future enemy it will regard us as the enemy now and respond by arming itself to the teeth. We should remember that one of the reasons for Japanese military expansion was because European fear of the Japanese lead to attempts to cut off Japan from the sources of raw materials and fuel that it needed for its economic growth. To break this virtual siege the Japanese launched the Greater Southeast Asia War.

A policy of trying to contain China might very well lead to the Chinese boosting their military capacity in order to match those of their potential enemy. History has taught us that when the military muscles are strong there is always a desire to flex them and to test their capacity. It requires but a minor incident for a full-scale conflagration to follow.

It is far better for China to be accepted as a major economic power. It will be powerful but it will not totally dominate the world. The U.S., Europe, Japan and even South Korea would provide a counterbalance. It is important to remember that China too is afraid. It is afraid of its traditional enemies in Asia and of the U.S. History has taught China that when it is weak it is likely to be ridden over roughshod by foreign powers. The unequal treaties of the past are still fresh in the minds of the Chinese.

Southeast Asia has the most to fear from China's expansionism. Unless China is provoked that fear is misplaced. In today's world military conquest is unnecessary, costly and counterproductive. We do not think that China would indulge in military adventures. There is therefore no reason for Southeast Asia to fear China's military might. But establishing a mechanism for defusing potentially dangerous disputes is necessary. The East Asian Economic Grouping can provide this mechanism.

China has assured Southeast Asia that the dispute over the Spratly islands can be resolved through negotiations. Southeast Asia should take China's words for this and begin serious discussion on a common stand over China's and each other's claims.

While military conquest or even threat is unlikely, economic domination is possible. It will not be total, but it can be sufficiently damaging for the economies of the Southeast Asian nations. But I have already pointed out that there are ways for Southeast Asia and others to counter this possibility.

The European Union is the product of the European Economic Community. The most significant achievement of the EEC is not so much economic as the half a century of peace that it brought to Europe. It is possible that the proposed EAEG will result in a similar peace for East Asia. And peace in East Asia can only be good for the region and for the rest of the world. Opposition to the EAEG is very difficult to understand. It cannot be that there is a wish to see East Asia remaining poor. It is very perplexing.

The EAEG will not become an East Asian Union as easily as the European countries, which in any case took a considerable length of time. For a long time the East Asian Group will remain a very loose grouping, confining itself to the discussion of regional affairs and common problems. Potential conflicts can be brought to meetings of the grouping at official, ministerial and Heads of Government level.

The proposal for an East Asia Monetary Fund as an extension of the swap arrangement can do harm to no one, within the grouping or outside it. Today's problem is likely to be financial and the fund should contribute towards earlier solutions when member countries get into financial difficulties.

As China will be a member of the EAEG, challenges posed by China that may be damaging to Southeast Asian countries can be discussed in the forum and mitigated. China surely realises that a prosperous and stable Southeast Asia is good for it. Poor countries are always a source of problems for rich neighbours. If the EAEG can contribute towards preventing China's challenge from damaging the economies of fellow members of the Grouping then China would surely want to listen and consider the effect of its challenge on the countries of Southeast Asia.

China will pose a challenge to Southeast Asian countries. But the EAEG would help resolve much of these problems. What remains would be opportunities for Southeast Asia to benefit from China's economic prosperity and stability. And these are enormous. Not only will China be a great market for the products and services of Southeast Asia but there will be a lot of Chinese investment in Southeast Asia. In addition with the passage of time the half a billion Southeast Asians will become a good market for China's products and services.

The only thing that the Southeast Asians need to worry is the attitude they take *vis-á-vis* China. If the Southeast Asians participate in trying to contain China then an atmosphere of confrontation will develop and much will be wasted on preparations for conflicts. Southeast Asia will certainly stand to lose in the ensuing tension.

But if Southeast Asia accepts the fact that China is there, that it cannot be wished away, that it is going to play its role in the economic development of East Asia and the world and accordingly look at China as we do Japan and South Korea, then, as much as Japan and South Korea have contributed towards the prosperity of Southeast Asia, China too will do the same.

China is both a challenge and an opportunity. This much is obvious. Whether we gain or lose because of the challenge and the opportunity offered by this new China very much depends on us the Southeast Asians.

We have a need to understand the problems posed by China and we can then design an approach that will minimise the challenge and maximise the opportunity.

This is my view. I may be wrong. But as the great Chinese leader Chou En-lai said, it is too early to tell.

Historically, China had not been a threat to Southeast Asia. The Chinese migrants who settled down in Southeast Asia tended to adopt the local language and much of the local culture. They remained Chinese however, but gradually lost touch with their relatives and clans in China. Although maintaining that Chinese anywhere were their people China had never sent gunboats to protect Chinese settlers in Southeast Asia. China never behaved like a metropolitan power nor tried to colonise Southeast Asian countries.

In the past, the small Southeast Asian states used to acknowledge the superior size of China by sending gold and silver flowers as gifts or tributes to the Emperor of China. But the submission was never more than that.

The emergence of China as an economic powerhouse should not worry Southeast Asian countries any more than in the past. There will be challenges and there will be opportunities. Faced with these the Southeast Asian countries will have to learn to manage the challenges and seize the opportunities. The chances are that at worse a balance will be attained but with astuteness Southeast Asia will benefit more from the opening up of the ever richer Chinese markets.

32

Asia in 2020: Challenges and Prospects

"There are today many cynics who find flaws in the entire Asean endeavour. God knows there are many flaws in Asean. Yet no one has ever said that Asean has not been a tremendous success in building a community of peace in what was once so often called 'a region in turmoil'."

AT the best of times, I think anyone who speaks with any degree of certainty about the future, especially about a future so distant as 2020, should be regarded as a charlatan. This is true at most times. If, even at the most stable of times, certainty is almost always a sure sign of an error in thinking, today it is the very height of naïvety—or utter ignorance.

A speech delivered at the Asean-India Business Luncheon in New Delhi, India, on October 17, 2002

It is especially true today, at a time of possible fundamental change, when history could take the world up a reasonable road to human progress or down the steep ravine to disaster.

We have today, because of the act of a small group of crazy extremists and the rage of an unfettered giant, the prospect of a radically new world; a new world unimaginable even a year and two months ago.

These preliminary remarks should suggest to you that while a positive mindset is essential for human achievement of any note—whether it is the running of a state or a corporation—our optimism must always be tampered by realism and the deliberate calculation not only of opportunity but also risk.

We should have no illusion about the possibility of the bleakest of futures for Asia. Our future could be as black as in the reasonably recent past.

I am sure I do not need to remind anyone in this room that the last few hundred years have been a period of shame for Asia. Our heads were bowed. For much of the time, we stood on our knees. Our people were impoverished. Our technological prowess was pathetic; our claim to civilisation completely tenuous.

Without a single exception, every nation in Asia, India included, has at one time or another over the last 50 years been given up as lost. We have been dismissed as basket cases, societies which can have no future. We have for some time now started to show the world what we can do. We have clearly turned the corner. We could be at the start of a peace and prosperity run that could take us to where we were, when we were the centre of human civilisation. We now have a historic opportunity to banish our period of shame and to put in its place, an era of pride.

While I do not know what exactly the future may bring, I have some very clear ideas about the objectives we must aggressively and relentlessly fight for in the years to come. I have some very clear ideas about some of the things we need to do, to make our future an era of pride. Let me begin with the objectives.

In the years ahead, it is obvious that there are a thousand and one things that we must keep our eye on. There are a hundred and one things that we must work at. But I believe that we must aggressively and relentlessly concentrate on two fundamental objectives.

First, we must in the years ahead build communities of durable peace and friendship. Second, we must ensure rapid and sustainable economic growth.

Let me begin with peace. This is where human progress begins. This is the first prerequisite. Let us never under-estimate the central importance of peace, true peace, which goes way beyond the mere absence of war. If in the years ahead we cannot secure true peace and sustain and strengthen it, I believe we do not have much of a future. If we are able to achieve this true and sustainable peace, we have a good chance of fulfilling the hopes and dreams of our people.

How is a warm and durable peace to be achieved? The first option is hegemony. The second is reliance on a military balance of power. The third is the option of community, of building regional relationships of reasonable mutual trust and reasonable mutual friendship, where no one is driven to rage, where cordiality takes the place of hate.

It wasn't so long ago that a "Pax Americana" over East Asia was spoken of in the fondest of ways in Washington and in some parts of East Asia under

American intellectual tutelage. Some of its advocates in Asia and further afield could not even understand why anyone in East Asia should have the slightest objection to American hegemony; although for some reason, when others in the region spoke of the virtues of a "Pax Nipponica", their blood pressure went up—and when others talked of a "Pax Sinica", their hair stood on ends. Somehow, an East Asia peace under the diktat of the U.S. was excellent but an East Asian peace under Japanese hegemony was choking and an East Asian peace under Chinese dominance was obscene.

Let us be clear about the imperial or hegemonic approach to peace. It is true that nothing is as powerful as an idea whose time has come. But it is also true that nothing is as powerless as an idea whose time has gone. Hegemony and imperialism, like the doctrine of "the divine right of kings" and "the mandate of heaven" are neither productive nor possible in today's world. The world today is too complicated and too democratic a place for imperialism to be a viable approach to true peace. It generates too much resentment and too much hate in too many hearts. 190 states with 6 billion people can be controlled. But million or two of them who can learn the rudiments of bomb-making over a weekend, cannot be easily controlled.

Those who fail to read the writings on the wall will pay the price for their political illiteracy. If hegemony is not tenable, why not that trusty old blunderbuss: the balance of power, and its small variant, the balance of terror?

An extreme form was well articulated by the ancient Romans who coined that famous adage: if you want peace, prepare for war. Less extreme models call for a counterbalancing of the enemy's military and other power. In many parts of East Asia, this was the dominant approach to the prevention of war in the 1940s, 1950s, 1960s, 1970s and 1980s. In East Asia today, it remains the dominant approach to peace and stability only in the Korean peninsula and perhaps across the Taiwan Straits. In the rest of Asia, it is no more prevalent.

Sometimes, of course, nations may face no other alternative but to rely on deterrence. But a balance of power approach is often a very costly approach because when you prepare for war, war all too often is what you get.

Modern armaments are getting ever more expensive. In the classic balance of power, arms races cannot be stopped; military budgets get too big (to the detriment of other national priorities); entrenched psychologies cannot change but get only further entrenched; nations and their people cannot relax; always, it is we versus "the enemy". The risks are of course heightened when nuclear weapons enter the balance of terror.

Rigid military balances of check and countercheck divert attention and energies from more important agendas and tend to freeze the status quo, when some accommodation, flexibility and progress may be good for all in the longer term. They are also a very low-aspiration approach because when balance of power systems work, at such substantial cost, all that you achieve is a cold and adversarial peace. Never a warm and cooperative peace.

Many will say that even in the period before September 11, it was already clearly a shoddy option. In the period after September 11, it is shoddier still because warfare has ceased to be the monopoly of the state and has become a tool of individuals and small groups too difficult to identify, still less to discipline. A cold and adversarial peace cannot secure the minimum level of security.

Many will of course say that the third option—achieving peace through building trust, relaxing tensions, building friendship and goodwill, a sense of community and a community of interest in peace—is idealistic. It is said to be difficult. It is said to be laborious. It is so demanding of patience and endless effort. They are right. But in the right conditions, peace through community is much more realistic than hegemony and the balance of power system—which can never achieve true peace. I believe that, despite all the obvious difficulties, it is still the most productive method for the creation of a warm and productive peace that is subservient to the welfare of the peoples of our nations.

Those who say that the community of friends approach to true peace is not possible have to explain the success of Western Europe, which twice in the last century brought a world war upon the entire world. Those who say that the community of friends approach is not possible must explain the success of Asean. And they should watch very closely the efforts at relaxing tensions and making friends in East Asia, the most turbulent, most war-prone region in the world in the generation after World War II.

After hundreds of years of enmity and fighting, who in Western Europe in 1945 could have imagined that this warring continent would be able to create a community of peace within just a generation? Whatever the success or failure of the economic community-building movement in Europe, no one can deny that the process of banishing war and building a true peace in that continent has been one of the wonders of the 20th century.

There are today many cynics who find flaws in the entire Asean endeavour. God knows there are many flaws in Asean. Yet no one has ever said that Asean has not been a tremendous success in building a community of peace in what was once so often called "a region in turmoil". Strangers have been turned into acquaintances. Acquaintances have been turned into comrades. Enemies have been turned into friends, not overnight; but still quite surprisingly fast.

To be sure, the new Asean members are not so chummy among themselves or with the older members. But there is no doubt that despite centuries of disdain, prejudice, animosity and pure hatred, no one in the entire region of Southeast Asia is preparing or even thinking of going to war against another. A community of cooperative peace has been established.

As for East Asia to the east of Bangladesh, let me remind the sceptics that 20 years ago China's new path was still uncertain and tenuous. Vietnam had just invaded Cambodia. Southeast Asia was divided into two camps. We were at daggers drawn. The East Asia of today is a very much different place.

History is a good teacher. It is good at teaching lessons. But history, especially our various conflicting interpretations of our past history, is not a good master. We must not be history's prisoners. And there is much to be said for breaking out of the deep dungeon of history. There is much to be said for burying the past and building the future together.

This is what Eastern Asia has done. And today, our highest priority is on generating economic dynamism and ensuring the welfare of our people by ensuring rapid and sustainable growth.

Because of our ability to secure peace and to concentrate on prosperity, over the last twenty and thirty years, the economies of East Asia have grown at rates unprecedented in human history. In Western Europe, the greatest age of economic dynamism was their Industrial Revolution. We in East Asia over the last generation have been able to grow at roughly twice the speed of Western Europe during its great Industrial Revolution.

It is very important for the rest of Asia that in the future India is part of our prosperity run; and it is very important that we run together. How do we do this? Many economists talk of the "East Asian model" of economic development. There are of course similarities that can be found in East Asia. We all have high levels of domestic savings, even though Malaysian and Chinese levels of domestic savings have been so historically high as to make the high-saving Japanese look like a nation of spendthrifts. We all have an obsession with education, although the incredible obsession that South Koreans and Taiwanese have with regard to education make the rest of us look like education-averse delinquents.

The truth is that there are many models of economic development in East Asia ranging from those economies which are very reliant on FDI to those like Japan and South Korea which are very reliant on domestic enterprises. Japan is much, much less dependent on exports than Malaysia or Singapore. South Korea developed on the basis of huge conglomerates called *chaebols* while Taiwan was built on small- and medium-scale enterprises.

What we all have in common is an awful lot of national pragmatism. We all did it according to the Sinatra Principle. We all did it our way. And the most important element was not the international system, or the regional system but the national pragmatism sans ideology.

In the days ahead, it seems clear enough that the most important helping hand that we all need is at the end of our own right arm. Our destinies are very much in our own hands. Almost always, no one can do to you worse than what you can do to yourself. Fortunately the obverse is also true. No one can do anything for you better than what you can do for yourself.

Having said this, let me stress one national policy that goes beyond the nation state that has proven to be productive of our individual national interests, one area where a concert of Asia is very much needed and one area where a partnership between India and Asean will be mutually beneficial.

In many parts of the world, beggar thy neighbour is a powerful reality, a natural policy response. If I can mention it, we in East Asia have found much value in prosper-thy-neighbour policies.

So many nations in East Asia have willy-nilly adopted this policy not because of altruism or idealism but because it has served their own enlightened national interest.

We all can choose our friends but we cannot choose our neighbours. A basic question we face is this: is it better to have neighbours which are impoverished, which cannot provide for their people, which are a hotbed of instability and turmoil; or is it better to have neighbours which are growing in prosperity, which can therefore buy more from you, which do not generate hordes of refugees and trouble makers who are likely to seek a haven in your country or cause havoc in your region?

It is of course not easy to sustain prosper-thy-neighbour policies when your neighbours are strange or different, when they might cause you so much trouble and inconvenience or say the wrong things about you and so often show no gratitude whatsoever. But I assure you that the returns are worth all the difficulty.

Secondly, let me stress the need for Asia to work together to shape the international economic system within which we have to work, which determine so much of our possibilities, over which presently we have so little influence, still less, control.

I have in the past been impressed so often by the posture taken by India in, for example, the WTO. India must continue to provide leadership on global economic issues and on the course and development of globalisation—which promised so much to all of humanity but which has been so selfishly hijacked by the greedy and the few in recent years.

Thirdly, let me suggest that it is high time for Asean and India to work on a comprehensive economic partnership that will be mutually beneficial to us and to the rest of Asia and the world.

There is today the Asean+3 process involving the ten Asean states, China, Japan and South Korea. This will develop because of its profound logic.

At the Asean summit in Brunei in November last year, President Jiang Zemin proposed and Asean leaders agreed to form an Asean-China Free Trade Area within ten years. Last month in Brunei, China and Asean agreed on an early harvest of tariff reduction in hundreds of items in eight agricultural areas to be implemented in the 2004-2006 period. A framework agreement is due to be signed by the leaders of Asean and China at the Summit Meeting to be held in Phnom

Penh next month. China and the Asean-5 (Indonesia, Malaysia, Philippines, Singapore and Thailand) are already a remarkably integrated trading area today. In the years ahead, we cannot but move closer together.

In Brunei last month, the economic ministers of Asean and Japan agreed to conclude an economic partnership agreement, including a free trade area, within ten years and to start its negotiation next year.

Also in Brunei, South Korea's economic minister suggested the idea of an Asean-South Korea Free Trade Area. For Asean, this should complete the logic of Asean free trade agreements in East Asia.

It would be interesting to see here, in India, how strong is the interest in an Asean-India Economic Partnership Agreement. In this case too, there is a profound economic logic.

I have mentioned already about history, about the past, and about the various versions of history that we all possess. Let me end by reiterating that history is a good teacher but a bad master. It must not be the jailer that keeps us confined within our damp dungeons. We must proceed from the present. And we should vigorously proceed from today to build the future together.

33

Malaysia Totally Committed to Asean

"I have had the privilege of attending most of the Asean Summits. During these years, I have seen many changes take place in Asean. Today, Asean encompasses the whole of Southeast Asia and it is one of the most successful regional organisations."

TO BE HONOURED by my fellow leaders in Asean is indeed something special. As you are all aware, this will be my last participation at the Asean Summit. The time has come for me to leave, after 22 years in office. I am grateful to all of you for your support, assistance, and above all friendship.

A speech delivered in response to President Megawati of Indonesia's farewell remarks during the 9th Asean Summit in Bali, Indonesia, on October 7, 2003

I have had the privilege of attending most of the Asean summits. During these years, I have seen many changes take place in Asean. Today, Asean encompasses the whole of Southeast Asia and it is one of the most successful regional organisations. Though in the early years, Asean was written off as an irrelevant organisation, we have proved that we are very relevant. How else can we explain the willingness of the countries of Northeast Asia and South Asia to hold dialogues with us. In fact, many outside the region have expressed the desire to be a member of Asean.

While Asean has made notable progress, we must not rest on our laurels. We need to address our challenges squarely. To address these challenges, we need to have the political will and commitment to continue to nurture and nourish Asean into an Asean Community. Here we can take a leaf from the process which led to the formation ultimately of the European Union. Malaysia, as one of the founding members of Asean, remains totally committed to Asean. Indeed, Asean will continue to be the cornerstone of Malaysia's foreign policy.

While Asean remains open and progressive, it must continue to deepen its relations with East Asia. An East Asian Community, with Asean at its core, is inevitable. It is important that we as Asean play our part to drive this cooperation in the right direction.

Finally, I wish to stress that as we move forward, we must not disregard nor erode the principles that have kept us together. The principles of non-interference, of consensus-based decision making, national and regional resilience, respect for national sovereignty, the renunciation of the threat or the use of force in the settlement of differences and disputes, must always be upheld by the Asean countries.

Finally may I take this opportunity to wish all my colleagues the best in their future undertakings. May Asean continue to flourish for the benefit of all our peoples and the peoples of this world.

Index

Dr Mahathir Mohamad has been prime minister of Malaysia since July 16, 1981. One of the most durable and outspoken figures on the world political stage, he first came to prominence in 1969 when he was expelled from the ruling party, UMNO, for writing a letter critical of the then-prime minister, Tunku Abdul Rahman. Before being readmitted to UMNO in 1972, he wrote his famous, highly controversial work, *The Malay Dilemma* (1970), which examined the economic backwardness of the Malays, and advocated state intervention to bring about their rehabilitation. The book was promptly banned in Malaysia. In *The Challenge* (1986), he explodes fallacies and exposes distortions concerning religion, education, democracy, communism, freedom and discipline, and the concerns of this world and the next. In *A New Deal for Asia* (1999), Dr Mahathir reflects on Malaysia's fight for independence and rails against those who blindly worship the free market.

As Malaysia's fourth prime minister, Dr Mahathir has played a pivotal role in the confident march of his people towards Vision 2020, his blueprint for Malaysia's advance towards fully developed status. Born on December 20, 1925, Dr Mahathir studied medicine in Singapore, where he met his future wife, Dr Siti Hasmah Mohd. Ali. After working as a doctor in government service, he left to set up his own private medical practice in his hometown, Alor Setar. In 1974, he gave that up to concentrate on his political career. Dr Mahathir and his wife have seven children and ten grandchildren.